THE TREE HOUSE BOOK

by DAVID STILES

designs & illustrations
by the author

AVON BOOKS

THE TREE HOUSE BOOK
IS AN ORIGINAL PUBLICATION
OF AVON BOOKS. THIS WORK
HAS NEVER BEFORE APPEARED
IN BOOK FORM.

AVON BOOKS
A division of
The Hearst Corporation
959 Eighth Avenue
New York, New York 10019

copyright © 1979 by David Stiles
Published by arrangement with
Library of Congress Catalog Number: 78-65887
ISBN: 0-380-43133-5

First Avon Printing, April, 1979
Third Printing
AVON TRADEMARK REG. U.S. PAT. OFF. AND IN
OTHER COUNTRIES, MARCA REGISTRADA, HECHO EN
U.S.A.

Printed in the U.S.A.

To my son — EBEN

TABLE of CONTENTS

Section I — GENERAL INFORMATION

Section II — THE FREE FORM TREE HOUSE

Section III — FOUR BASIC DESIGNS

Section IV = Miscellaneous

SECTION I

General information you should
know before starting to
build a tree house.

INTRODUCTION

IF YOU THINK TREE HOUSES ARE JUST FOR KIDS, YOU ARE WRONG. THERE ARE AN INCREASINGLY LARGE NUMBER OF ADULTS BUILDING TREE HOUSES TO LIVE IN YEAR ROUND, OR TO SPEND SPECIAL WEEKENDS GETTING AWAY FROM IT ALL. THERE USED TO BE AN ELDERLY BOHEMIAN COUPLE IN GREENWICH VILLAGE (NEW YORK CITY) WHO LIVED IN A TREE HOUSE BACK IN THE '30's.

IF YOU HAVE BOUGHT SOME PROPERTY IN THE COUNTRY AND ARE WONDERING JUST HOW TO POSITION YOUR HOUSE IN RELATION TO THE SUN, OR IF YOU ARE WAITING FOR A BUILDING LOAN TO COME THROUGH, WHY NOT TRY LIVING IN A TREE HOUSE FIRST? YOU MAY DECIDE YOU DON'T REALLY NEED AN EXPENSIVE HOUSE AFTER ALL.

I AM TOLD OF A SECRET COMMUNITY OF TREE HOUSES ON THE COAST OF CALIFORNIA, RESPLENDENT WITH ELECTRICITY AND PLUMBING, UNKNOWN TO THE LOCAL BUILDING INSPECTOR AND TAX COLLECTOR.

THE TREE HOUSES SHOWN IN THIS BOOK ARE PURPOSELY MADE SIMPLE SO A CHILD COULD BUILD THEM; HOWEVER THE BASIC TECHNIQUES ARE APPLICABLE TO MUCH LARGER STRUCTURES. SINCE EVERY TREE VARIES IN SIZE AND SHAPE, IT IS IMPOSSIBLE TO GIVE SPECIFIC DIMENSIONS. THE DRAWINGS SHOULD GIVE YOU A GOOD IDEA OF THE VARIOUS CONSTRUCTION METHODS NECESSARY TO MAKE YOUR PARTICULAR TREE HOUSE. THE DESIGNS CAN BE CHANGED AND ELABORATED ON ACCORDING TO YOUR INDIVIDUAL TASTE. THE ONLY FIRM RULES ARE THAT YOUR TREE HOUSE BE FUN, INVENTIVE, AND SAFE.

WHERE TO BUILD ?

IF YOU ARE CONSIDERING BUILDING IN YOUR BACKYARD ALSO CONSIDER YOUR NEIGHBOR. USE THE GRID PAPER IN THE BACK OF THIS BOOK TO MAKE A ROUGH SKETCH AND SHOW IT TO THEM FOR THEIR APPROVAL. POINT OUT THE TREE ON WHICH YOU PLAN TO BUILD AND ASK THEIR ADVICE. (YOU DON'T HAVE TO FOLLOW IT.)

The empty lot down the street? If so, be ready for the unknown owner to suddenly make himself, and his feelings about your trespassing on his property, known. Be prepared to tear down your hard work if he objects to it.

The woods? Somebody always owns the woods whether it be the "feds," the state, or the real estate investors. If YOU don't own it, try to find out who does, and ask their permission. They may love the idea and use it to show their clients the feasibility of building there. Or, if you're feeling adventuresome, build it back far enough so no one will ever discover it. Just remember, tree houses stand out like sore thumbs in the fall when the leaves disappear.

<u>WHERE TO FIND WOOD</u> is the next big consideration. The most obvious and economical source is the natural dead wood, (logs, branches, etc.) found lying in the woods. Never chop down live trees to make a tree house. Even though it's difficult to find long straight logs in the woods unless you have unlimited acreage; a tree house made out of logs always looks best.

The other source is scrap wood from a new house site which any "nice" builder will probably agree to give you since chances are his scrap pile will eventually have to be burned or hauled away. He may also have some scrap roofing and building paper to give you. Also, check the lumber yards for scrap wood as they often have quantities of wood they

ARE THROWING AWAY. IF YOU HAVE TO BUY LUMBER, ASK AT
THE LUMBER YARD IF THEY HAVE ANY LOW GRADE LUMBER
SUITABLE FOR SCAFFOLDING. QUITE OFTEN LUMBER YARDS
SELL GRAY OR WEATHERED LUMBER AT A CHEAP PRICE.
THIS TYPE OF WOOD WOULD SERVE YOUR NEEDS PERFECTLY.
WHATEVER TYPE OF LUMBER YOU USE, MAKE SURE IT DOESN'T
HAVE TOO MANY KNOTS IN ANY ONE AREA AS THIS MAY
SERIOUSLY WEAKEN THE WOOD.

SOMETIMES YOU CAN FIND A NEIGHBOR WHO HAS A
SHED HE WANTS TO GET RID OF, AND YOU CAN OFFER TO
TEAR IT DOWN IN RETURN FOR THE WOOD.

APPEARANCE

ALTHOUGH THIS IS UP TO YOU, IT IS WISE
TO ALSO CONSIDER YOUR NEIGHBORS. THEY HAVE GOOD REASON
TO OBJECT IF YOUR TREE HOUSE IS STARTED WITH ALL GOOD
INTENTIONS BUT LEFT UNFINISHED, AFFORDING THEM A VIEW OF
AWKWARD ANGLED BOARDS SILHOUETTED AGAINST THE SKY.
THE BEST SOLUTION FOR ALL CONCERNED IS TO SITUATE YOUR
TREE HOUSE SO IT IS AS INVISIBLE AS POSSIBLE. UNLESS YOU
ARE REPRODUCING A "VICTORIAN GINGERBREAD" HOUSE, IT
IS ADVISABLE NOT TO PAINT. LET IT WEATHER TO LOOK LIKE
PART OF THE TREE.

SECURITY

IT IS NOT ADVISABLE TO PUT A LOCK
ON A TREE HOUSE DOOR. THIS PRESENTS AN IRRESISTIBLE
CHALLENGE TO NEIGHBORHOOD KIDS TO TRY AND BREAK IN -
AND THEY WILL PROBABLY SUCCEED. IF YOU MUST HAVE
REAL WINDOWS, MAKE THEM OUT OF UNBREAKABLE CLEAR
LEXAN PLASTIC. AT ANY RATE, IT IS MORE IN THE SPIRIT
OF TREE HOUSES TO KEEP THEM OPEN, WELCOMING ALL
VISITORS. (SEE TEAR-OUT SIGN ON PAGE 71.)

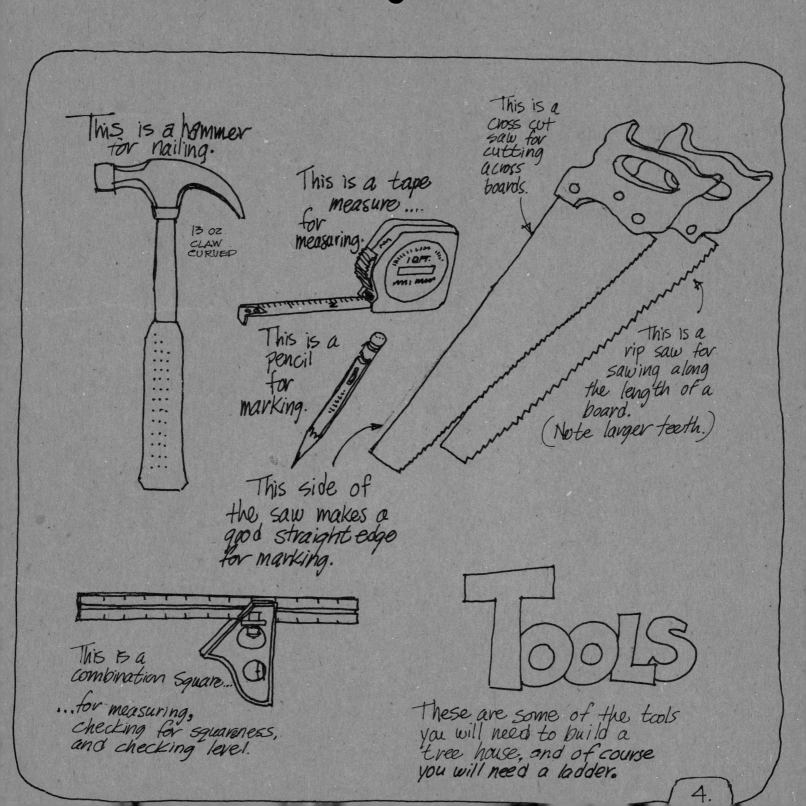

This is a hammer for nailing.

13 OZ. CLAW CURVED

This is a tape measure .... for measuring.

This is a pencil for marking.

This side of the saw makes a good straight edge for marking.

This is a cross cut saw for cutting across boards.

This is a rip saw for sawing along the length of a board. (Note larger teeth.)

This is a combination square... ...for measuring, checking for squareness, and checking level.

TOOLS

These are some of the tools you will need to build a tree house, and of course you will need a ladder.

4.

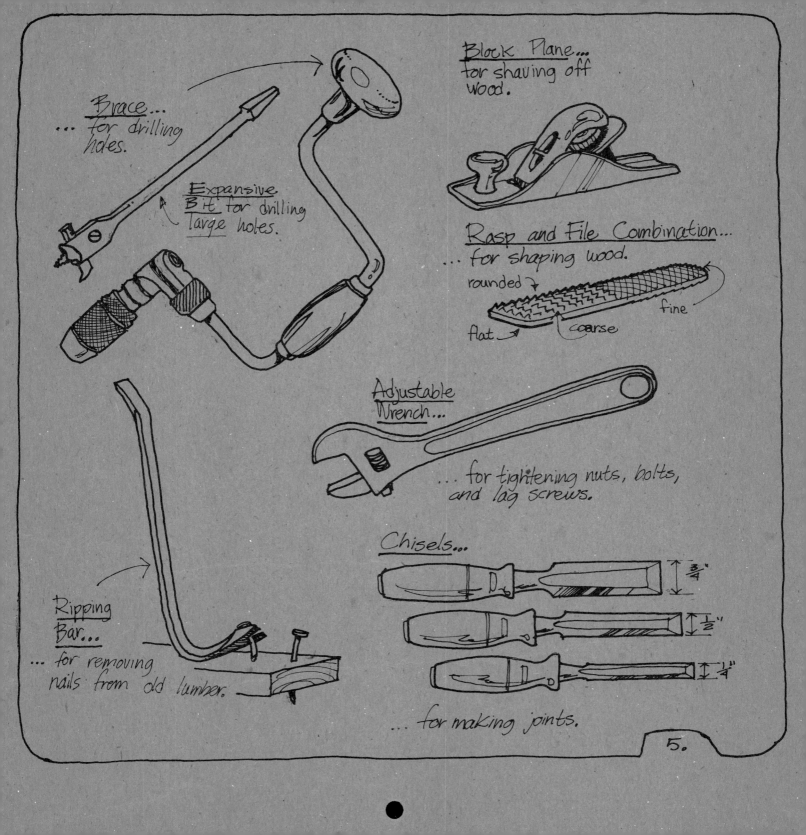

Brace... ... for drilling holes.

Expansive Bit for drilling large holes.

Block Plane... for shaving off wood.

Rasp and File Combination... ... for shaping wood.

rounded →

flat →   coarse   fine

Adjustable Wrench... ... for tightening nuts, bolts, and lag screws.

Ripping Bar... ... for removing nails from old lumber.

Chisels...

$\frac{3}{4}$"

$I\frac{1}{2}$"

$I\frac{1}{4}$"

... for making joints.

5.

NAILS, BOLTS, SCREWS

Common Nails

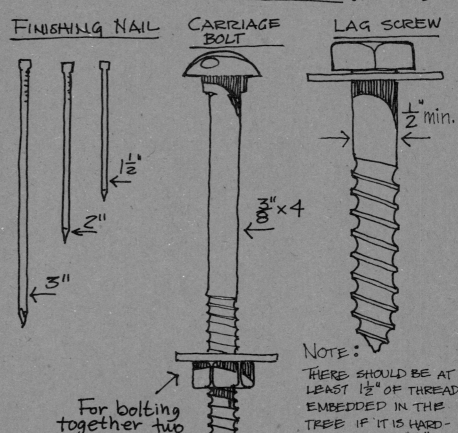

← 2"

← 3 1/4"

← 4 1/2"

Here are some nails, bolts, and screws that you are most likely to use. Make sure that they are all <u>galvanized</u> (coated).

Finishing Nail

← 1 1/2"

← 2"

← 3"

Carriage Bolt

← 3" × 4

For bolting together two beams.

Lag Screw

1/2" min.

Note:

There should be at least 1 1/2" of thread embedded in the tree if it is hardwood and 2 1/2" of thread embedded in the tree if it is softwood.

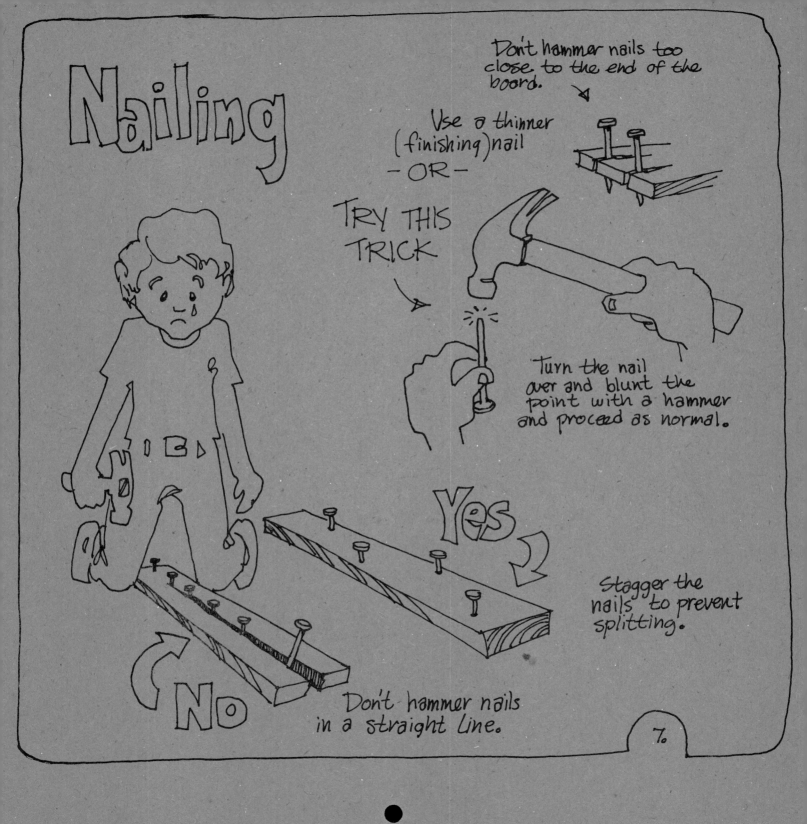

TOE NAILING

BEAMS TO BRANCHES

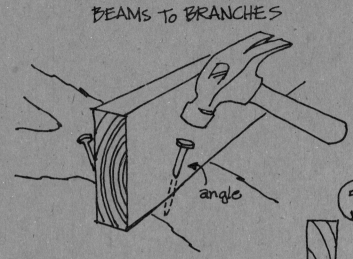

angle

HINT

Bent nails are actually better for this particular job — OR — Try starting the nail at an angle, bending it down, and finish nailing.

① ② ③

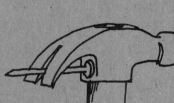

When the place you want to nail is out of reach —

Wedge a nail into the claws of the hammer and start the nail with one blow while holding on to a support with your other hand!

Before trying to nail a board up into a tree — start the nails on the ground so that the points are sticking out the other side...

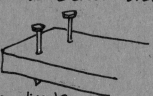

Then climb the tree and nail it on.

One board steps are BAD...

because the step can either pull out or pivot.

STEPS...
... should be checked regularly each year and tested by tying a rope to the step and pulling down hard while standing on the ground.

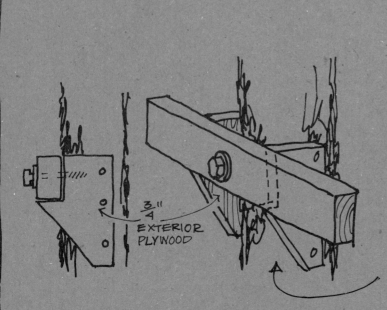

3/4"
EXTERIOR PLYWOOD

A better way to make steps is to cut up exterior plywood sheathing (generally found in scrap piles where new houses are being built). Cut the plywood into side brackets, as shown here, and nail them to the tree. The step rests in the notch and is screwed into the tree with a heavy lag screw.

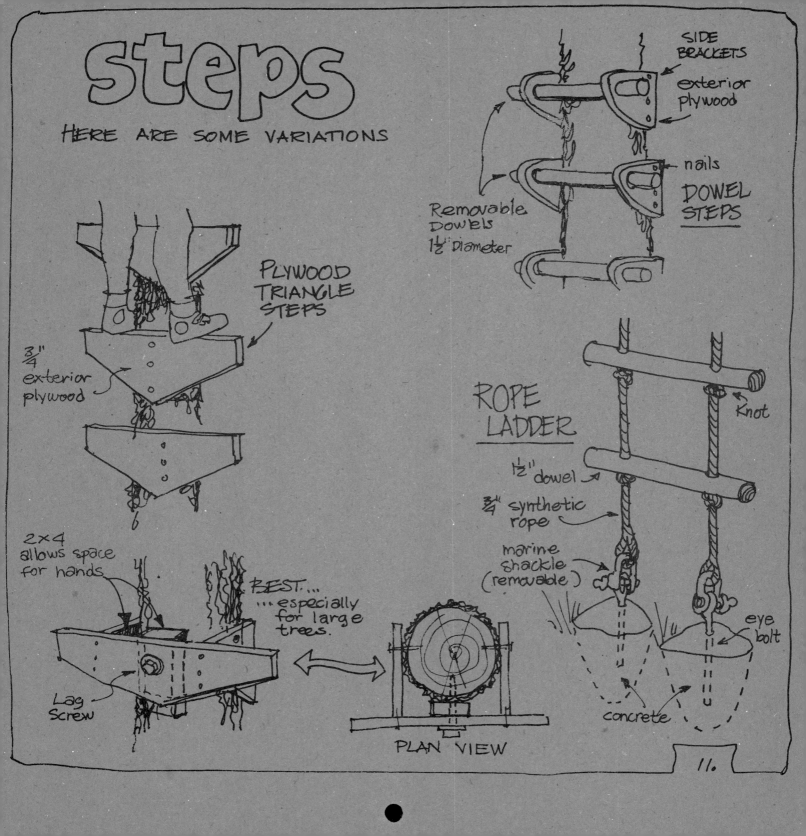

steps

HERE ARE SOME VARIATIONS

SIDE BRACKETS

exterior plywood

nails

DOWEL STEPS

Removable Dowels 1½" Diameter

PLYWOOD TRIANGLE STEPS

¾" exterior plywood

ROPE LADDER

Knot

1½" dowel

¾" synthetic rope

marine shackle (removable)

eye bolt

concrete

2×4 allows space for hands

BEST... ...especially for large trees.

Lag Screw

PLAN VIEW

more steps

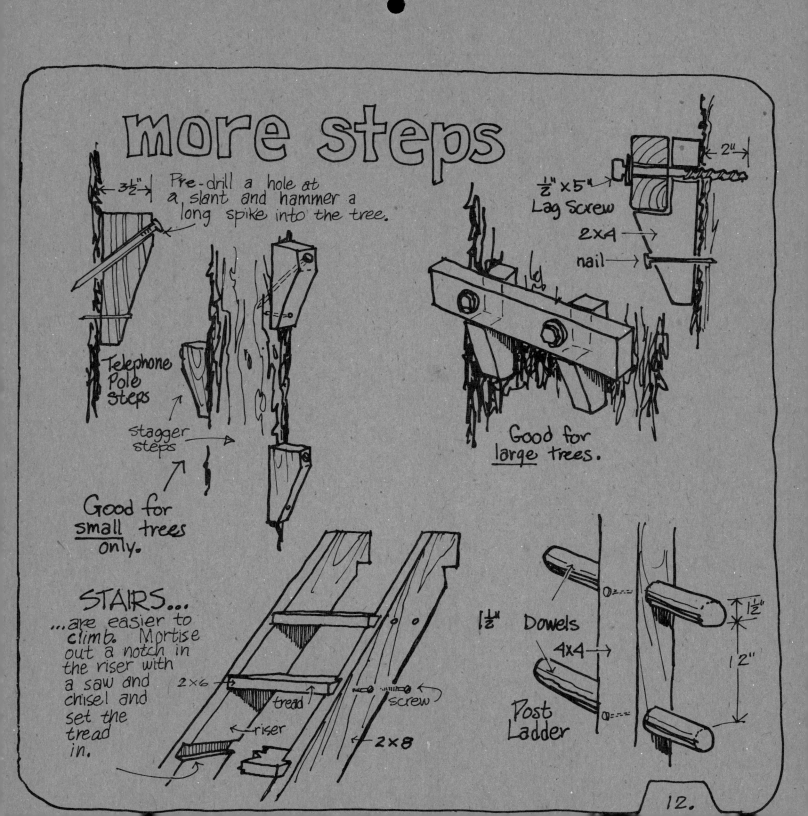

$3\frac{1}{2}"$

Pre-drill a hole at a slant and hammer a long spike into the tree.

Telephone Pole steps

stagger steps

Good for __small__ trees only.

$\frac{1}{2}" \times 5"$ Lag Screw

2×4

nail

2"

Good for __large__ trees.

STAIRS...
...are easier to climb. Mortise out a notch in the riser with a saw and chisel and set the tread in.

2×6

tread

riser

screw

2×8

$1\frac{1}{2}"$ Dowels

4×4

$1\frac{1}{2}"$

12"

Post Ladder

Safety Aloft

Be careful when removing nails from trees. Always keep one arm around something stationary and use a rope safety harness tied around your waist. (next page)

To Remove Nails...
Use a wrecking bar or pry bar for more leverage.

Use a block under the hammer head to remove stubborn nails.

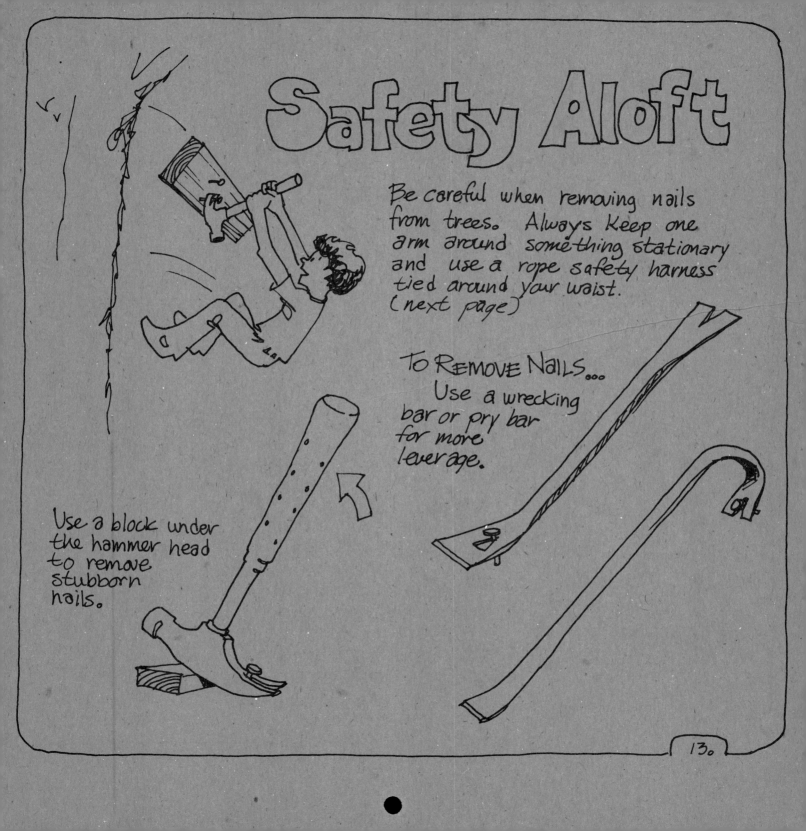

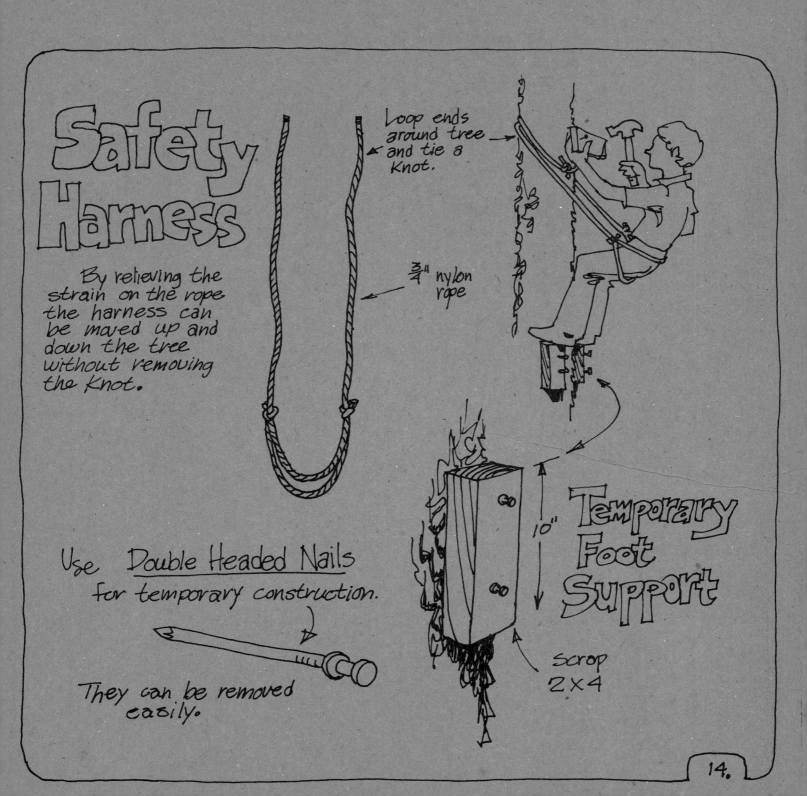

Safety Harness

By relieving the strain on the rope the harness can be moved up and down the tree without removing the knot.

Loop ends around tree and tie a knot.

3/4" nylon rope

Use **Double Headed Nails** for temporary construction.

They can be removed easily.

Temporary Foot Support

10"

scrap 2 × 4

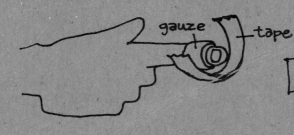
gauze — tape

FIRST AID

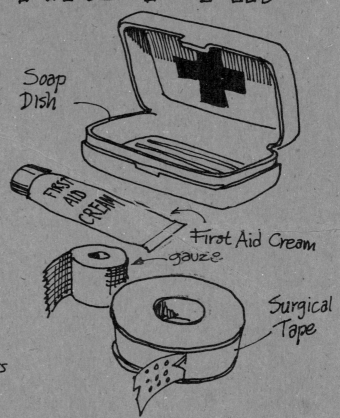

Make this small first aid kit from a soap dish and stock it with these items:

Soap Dish

First Aid Cream

gauze

Surgical Tape

Scissors

Tweezers
for removing splinters

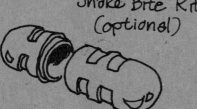

Snake Bite Kit
(optional)

Make Your Own Bandages

You can make better bandages than you can buy at a store. They will cost less, stay on longer, and can be tailor made to fit any part of your body.

SECTION II

The Free Form Tree House

TWO APPROACHES TO BUILDING A TREE HOUSE

THE FIRST APPROACH IS TO CARRY A BUNCH OF BOARDS UP INTO A VERY LARGE TREE AND START NAILING THEM ONTO THE TREE WHEREVER THERE ARE TWO BRANCHES AT THE SAME LEVEL. THIS APPROACH REQUIRES NO SPECIFIC PLAN AT ALL, RATHER IT USES THE TREE TO SUGGEST THE DESIGN OF THE STRUCTURE. IT IS A VERY SPONTANEOUS, CREATIVE WAY TO BUILD A TREE HOUSE. ITS MAIN PROBLEM IS FINDING A WAY TO BUILD A LEVEL PLATFORM. WAYS OF DEALING WITH THIS, AND OTHER PROBLEMS THAT CONFRONT THE "FREE FORM" TREE HOUSE BUILDER, ARE DETAILED IN THE NEXT FEW PAGES. IF YOU ARE AN INVENTIVE TYPE OF PERSON WHO LIKES TO DIVE INTO A PROJECT AND DEAL WITH PROBLEMS AS THEY ARISE, THEN THIS IS THE APPROACH FOR YOU.

THE SECOND APPROACH IS FOR THOSE WHO LIKE TO KNOW WHAT THEY ARE DOING BEFORE THEY BEGIN. IT TAKES INTO CONSIDERATION THE MOST TYPICAL SITUATIONS THAT YOU ARE MOST LIKELY TO FIND, NAMELY: ONE TREE TO BUILD IN, TWO TREES TO BUILD IN, THREE TREES TO BUILD IN, AND, FOUR TREES TO BUILD IN. IN EACH CASE I HAVE GIVEN A SPECIFIC DESIGN THAT YOU CAN FOLLOW IN STEP-BY-STEP FASHION ACCORDING TO THE NUMBER AND GROUPING OF TREES AVAILABLE TO YOU. THESE FOUR BASIC DESIGNS ARE SHOWN IN SECTION III.

THE FREE FORM TREE HOUSE

CHOOSING THE RIGHT TREE

BEGIN BY STUDYING THE TREES AVAILABLE TO YOU. WALK AROUND THEM AND SCRUTINIZE THEM CAREFULLY FROM ALL ANGLES WHILE TAKING INTO ACCOUNT THESE FOUR CONSIDERATIONS:

1. <u>IS THE TREE STRONG ENOUGH</u> TO HOLD A TREE HOUSE? IF YOU ARE USING ONLY ONE TREE, THEN THE TREE SHOULD BE AT LEAST 1 FOOT THICK AT THE BASE. IF YOU ARE USING SEVERAL TREES, THEY SHOULD BE AT LEAST 8 INCHES THICK.

2. <u>IS THE TREE DEAD</u>, OR ARE THERE ANY DEAD BRANCHES THAT MIGHT FALL DOWN IN A WIND-STORM AND DAMAGE THE TREE HOUSE? IT IS EASY TO TELL DEAD TREES IN THE SUMMER DUE TO THEIR LACK OF GREEN LEAVES, BUT IN THE WINTER LOOK FOR BUDS ON THE ENDS OF THEIR BRANCHES AS A SIGN THAT THEY ARE ALIVE.

3. <u>DISTANCE FROM A HOUSE</u> IS AN IMPORTANT CONSIDERATION IF YOU ARE PLANNING TO USE ELECTRIC TOOLS TO BUILD WITH. IF THE TREE YOU CHOOSE IS TOO FAR FOR AN ELECTRIC EXTENSION CORD, YOU CAN PERHAPS PRE-DRILL SOME OF THE LARGE HOLES BEFORE CARRYING YOUR LUMBER TO THE TREE. IF THIS IS NOT FEASIBLE, YOU CAN RENT OR BUY A CORDLESS BATTERY

CONT. NEXT PAGE

OPERATED DRILL. (BLACK & DECKER MAKES A GOOD ONE.)

4. <u>HOW HIGH FROM THE GROUND</u> SHOULD A TREE HOUSE BE? BEFORE YOU BUILD YOUR TREE HOUSE IN THE TOP OF THE TALLEST TREE, BEAR IN MIND THAT THE GREATEST CHANCE OF FALLING OUT OF THE TREE HOUSE OCCURS WHEN YOU ARE BUILDING IT. IT IS VERY DIFFICULT TO HOLD A HAMMER IN ONE HAND, HOLD A BOARD IN ANOTHER, HOLD A NAIL IN THE THIRD, AND HOLD ON TO THE TREE WITH A FOURTH HAND. THE ANSWER IS TO BUILD CLOSE ENOUGH TO THE GROUND SO THAT YOU CAN REACH IT, WHILE STANDING ON THE GROUND. YOU WILL STILL GET A LOFTY FEELING OF EUPHORIA WHEN PERCHED ONLY SIX FEET IN THE AIR.

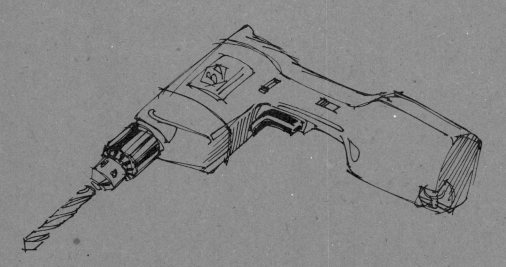

Look for a strong, live tree with thick branches reaching out close to the ground.

PLANNING A
TREE HOUSE
IN YOUR
MIND

WHILE LOOKING AT A
TREE TRY TO IMAGINE YOUR
ARMS ARE BRANCHES HOLDING
A LARGE BOX ▫ THEN TRY
TO IMAGINE WHICH BRANCHES
IN THE TREE A LARGE BOX
WOULD REST ON AND BUILD
YOUR TREE HOUSE THERE ▫

The Platform

THE MOST IMPORTANT PART OF BUILDING A TREE HOUSE IS ERECTING A STRONG, LEVEL PLATFORM IN THE TREE. ONCE THIS IS DONE, THE REST GOES QUITE EASILY.

THE WAY TO DO THIS IS TO CLIMB UP INTO THE TREE WITH A LIGHT 1X2 STICK AND A LEVEL. REST THE STICK ACROSS TWO BRANCHES WHERE YOU WANT THE TREE HOUSE TO BE, AND CHECK TO SEE IF IT'S LEVEL. CHANCES ARE IT WON'T BE! TO GET AROUND THIS PROBLEM YOU WILL HAVE TO CONSTRUCT SPECIAL SUPPORTS ON WHICH PLATFORM BEAMS WILL REST. BEAR IN MIND THAT YOU WILL NEED AT LEAST 3 LEVEL POINTS ON WHICH TO REST THE TREE HOUSE. ONE OF THESE POINTS MIGHT BE THE TREE TRUNK ITSELF. THE OTHERS MIGHT HAVE TO BE BUILT UP FROM THE BRANCHES AS SHOWN HERE.

THREE WAYS TO ADJUST
THE LEVEL OF THE PLATFORM

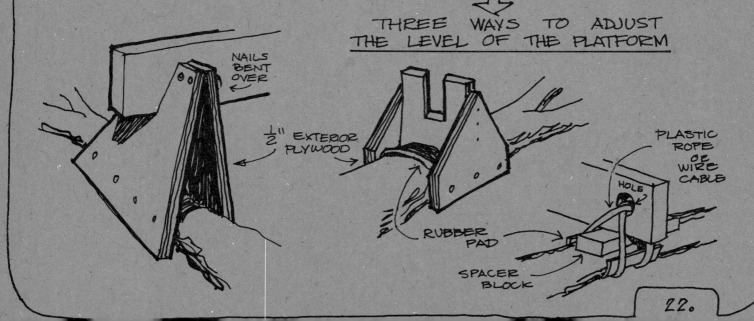

NAILS BENT OVER

½" EXTERIOR PLYWOOD

RUBBER PAD

PLASTIC ROPE OR WIRE CABLE

HOLE

SPACER BLOCK

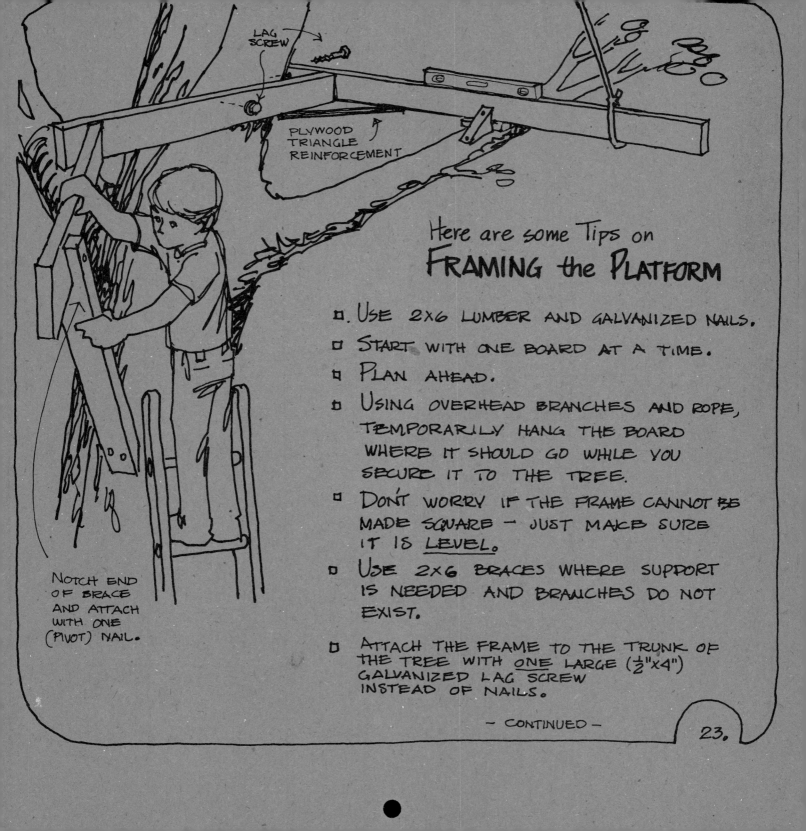

LAG
SCREW

PLYWOOD
TRIANGLE
REINFORCEMENT

NOTCH END
OF BRACE
AND ATTACH
WITH ONE
(PIVOT) NAIL.

Here are some Tips on FRAMING the PLATFORM

▫. USE 2x6 LUMBER AND GALVANIZED NAILS.

▫ START WITH ONE BOARD AT A TIME.

▫ PLAN AHEAD.

▫ USING OVERHEAD BRANCHES AND ROPE, TEMPORARILY HANG THE BOARD WHERE IT SHOULD GO WHILE YOU SECURE IT TO THE TREE.

▫ DON'T WORRY IF THE FRAME CANNOT BE MADE SQUARE — JUST MAKE SURE IT IS <u>LEVEL</u>.

▫ USE 2x6 BRACES WHERE SUPPORT IS NEEDED AND BRANCHES DO NOT EXIST.

▫ ATTACH THE FRAME TO THE TRUNK OF THE TREE WITH <u>ONE</u> LARGE ($\frac{1}{2}$"x4") GALVANIZED LAG SCREW INSTEAD OF NAILS.

— CONTINUED —

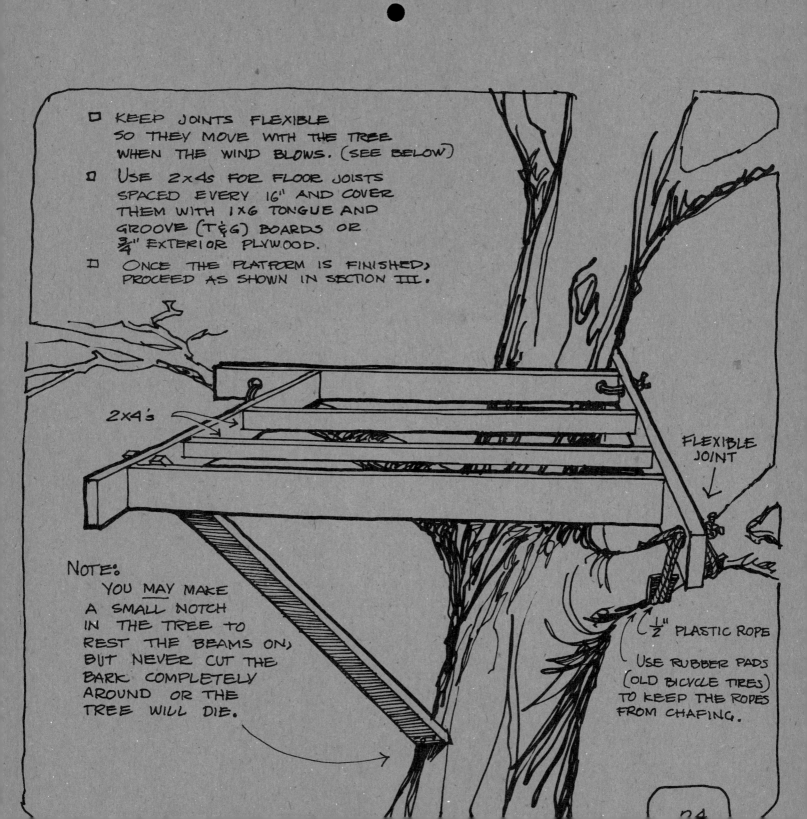

□ KEEP JOINTS FLEXIBLE
SO THEY MOVE WITH THE TREE
WHEN THE WIND BLOWS. (SEE BELOW)

□ USE 2x4s FOR FLOOR JOISTS
SPACED EVERY 16" AND COVER
THEM WITH 1x6 TONGUE AND
GROOVE (T&G) BOARDS OR
¾" EXTERIOR PLYWOOD.

□ ONCE THE PLATFORM IS FINISHED,
PROCEED AS SHOWN IN SECTION III.

2x4's

FLEXIBLE
JOINT

NOTE:
YOU MAY MAKE
A SMALL NOTCH
IN THE TREE TO
REST THE BEAMS ON,
BUT NEVER CUT THE
BARK COMPLETELY
AROUND OR THE
TREE WILL DIE.

½" PLASTIC ROPE

USE RUBBER PADS
(OLD BICYCLE TIRES)
TO KEEP THE ROPES
FROM CHAFING.

SECTION III

Four Basic Designs That You Can Build

1. A Tree House Built on One Tree

2. A Tree House Built on Two Trees

3. A Tree House Built on Three Trees

4. A Tree House Built on Four Trees
(or two trees and two posts)

25.

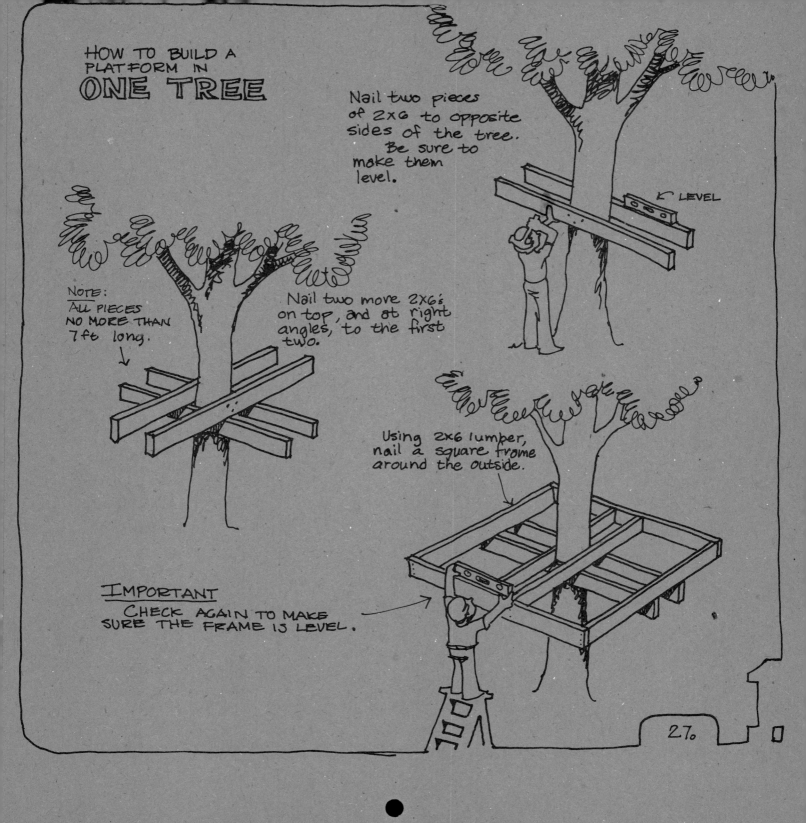

HOW TO BUILD A PLATFORM IN
ONE TREE

Nail two pieces of 2x6 to opposite sides of the tree. Be sure to make them level.

LEVEL

NOTE:
ALL PIECES NO MORE THAN 7 ft long.

Nail two more 2x6's on top, and at right angles, to the first two.

Using 2x6 lumber, nail a square frame around the outside.

IMPORTANT
CHECK AGAIN TO MAKE SURE THE FRAME IS LEVEL.

27.

CORNER BRACES

Cut the four braces (out of 2x4) to fit the corners as shown in this sketch.

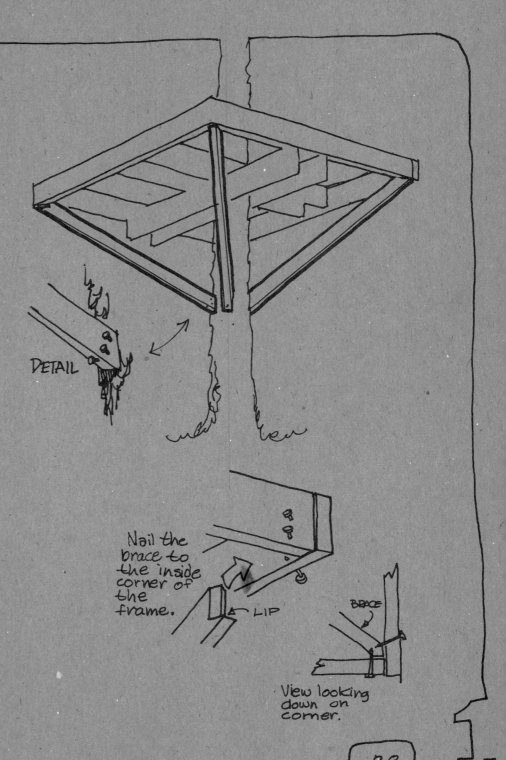

DETAIL

Make these two angle cuts...

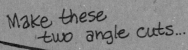

45°

90°

...then cut off CORNERS to form a lip.

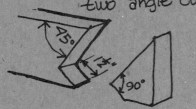

45°

↑ Lip

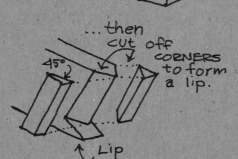

↑ Lip

Nail the brace to the inside corner of the frame.

← LIP

BRACE

View looking down on corner.

THE FLOOR

Fill in between the outer frame with 2x4 bridges so that there is no space larger than 16".

FLOORING

Use exterior plywood or scrap boards of uniform thickness.

DON'T FORGET THE DOORWAY. FRAME IT with 2x4 and construct the floor around it.

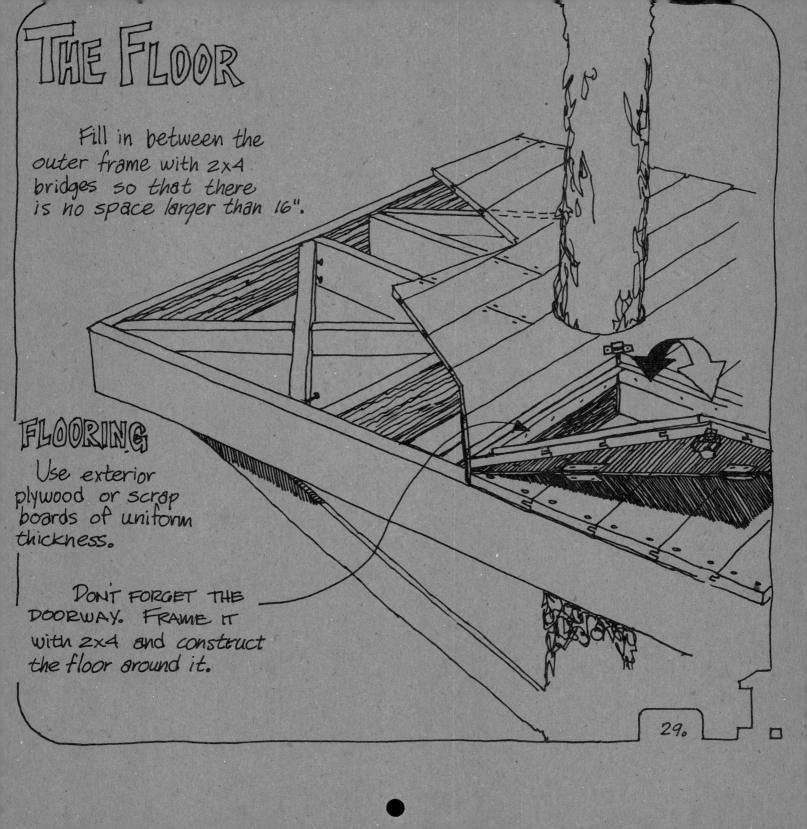

29.

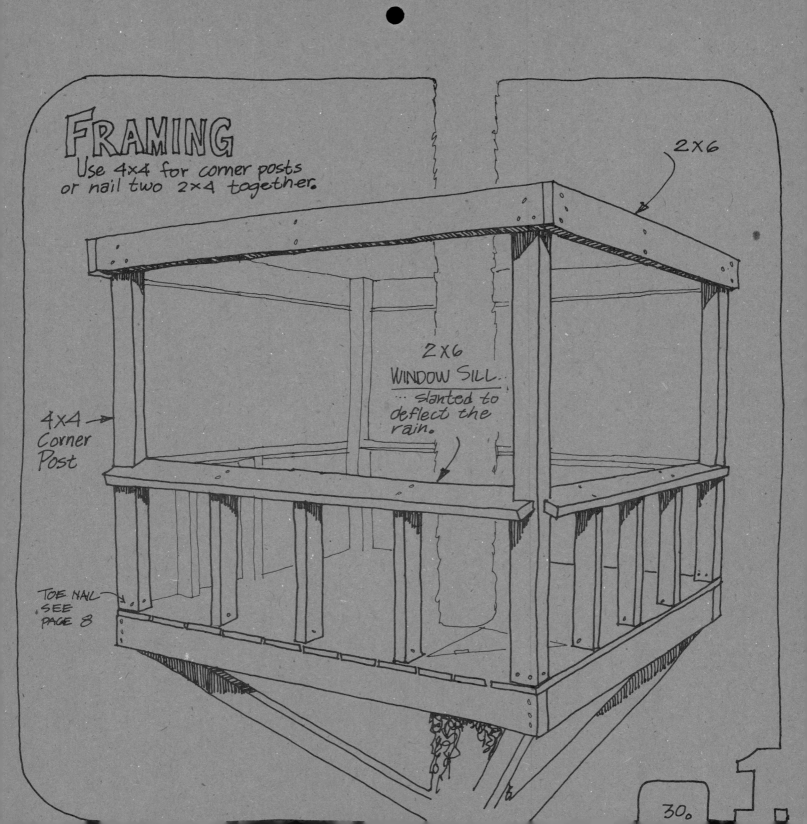

FRAMING
Use 4x4 for corner posts
or nail two 2x4 together.

2x6

2x6
WINDOW SILL.
... slanted to
deflect the
rain.

4x4
Corner
Post

TOE NAIL
SEE
PAGE 8

30.

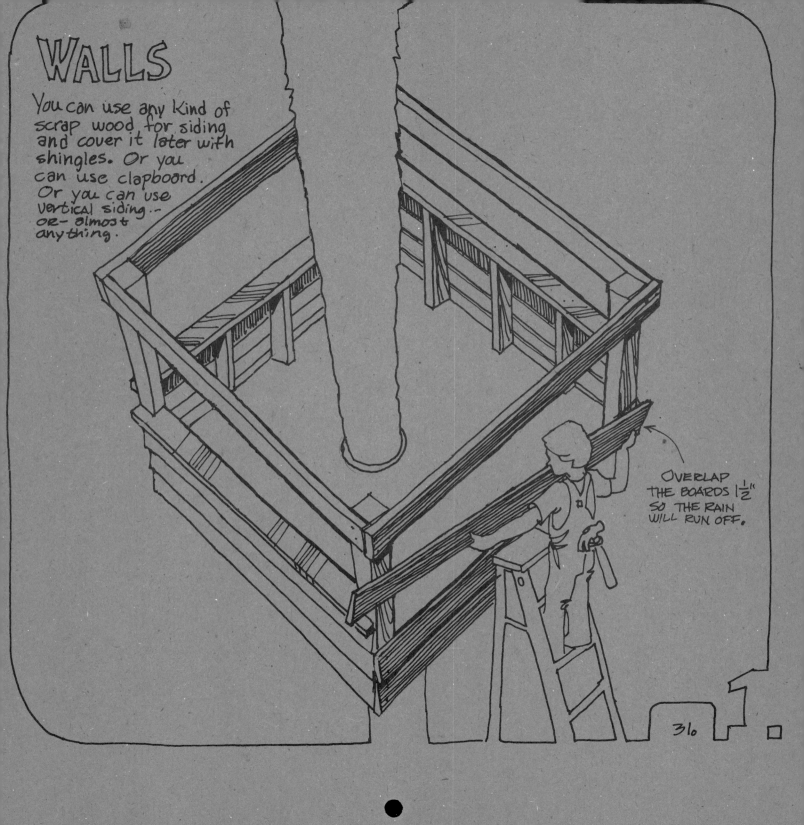

WALLS

You can use any kind of scrap wood for siding and cover it later with shingles. Or you can use clapboard. Or you can use vertical siding — or — almost anything.

OVERLAP THE BOARDS 1½" SO THE RAIN WILL RUN OFF.

36

ROOF FRAME

Put up the corner rafters first, and then the ones in between.

Nail 1x4 across the rafters to provide a surface for the final roof covering.

SEE PAGE 58 FOR ROOF DETAILS.

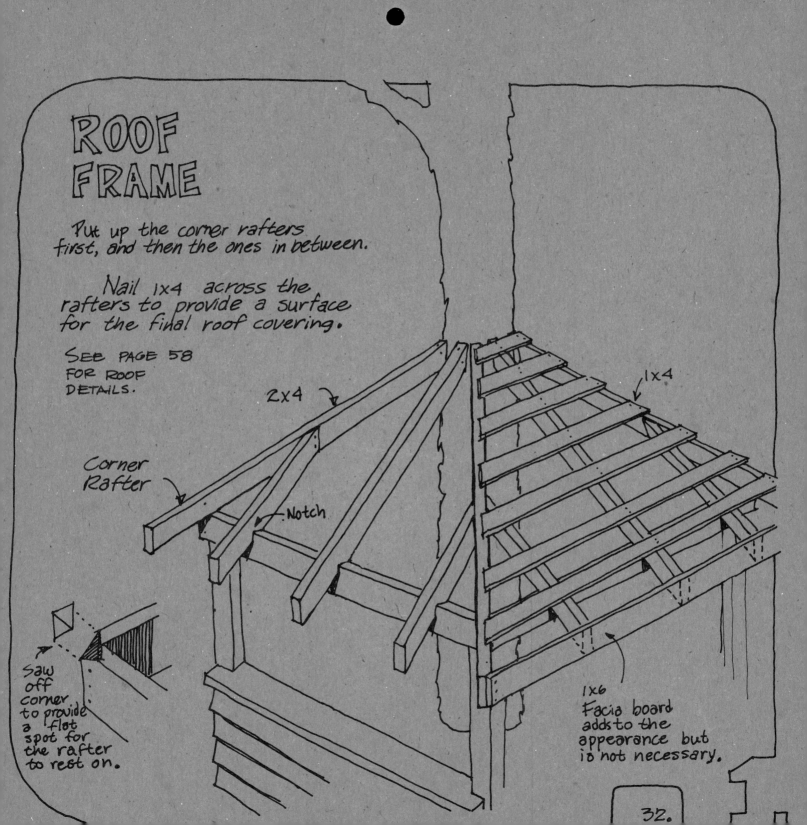

2x4

Corner Rafter

Notch

1x4

Saw off corner to provide a flat spot for the rafter to rest on.

1x6 Facia board adds to the appearance but is not necessary.

2
TREES

33.
2

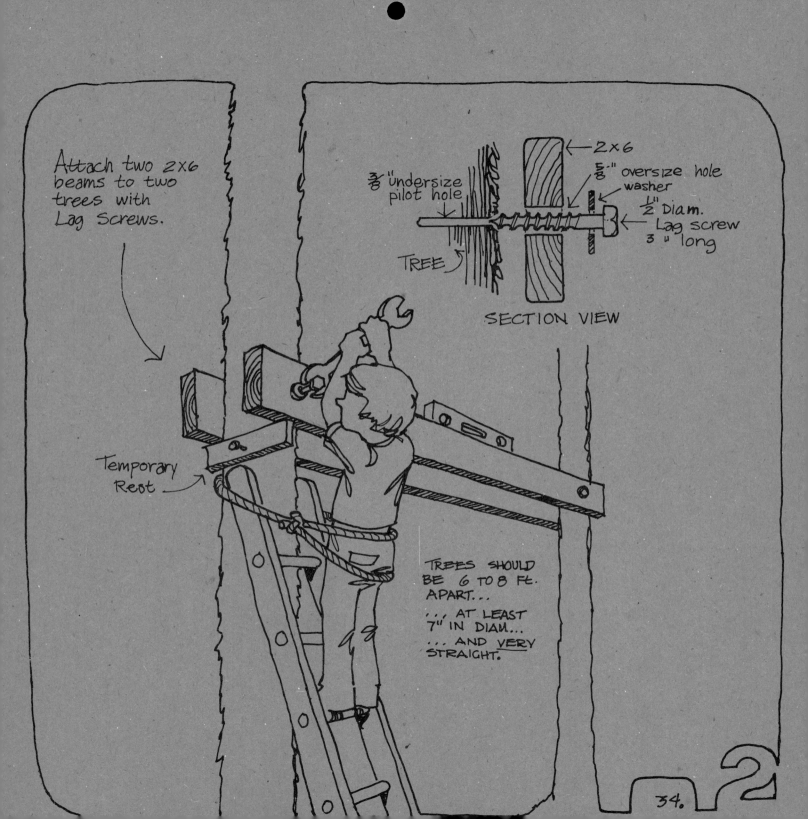

Attach two 2x6 beams to two trees with Lag Screws.

Temporary Rest

2x6

3/8" undersize pilot hole

5/8" oversize hole washer

1/2" Diam. Lag screw 3" long

TREE

SECTION VIEW

TREES SHOULD BE 6 TO 8 FT. APART...

...AT LEAST 7" IN DIAM...

...AND VERY STRAIGHT.

Triangles

CUT SIX PIECES OF 2×4 SIX FEET LONG AND BUILD TWO TRIANGULAR FRAMES.

ON THE TWO BOTTOM CORNERS OF EACH TRIANGLE DRILL $\frac{1}{2}$" DIAM. HOLE IN THE CENTER OF EACH PIECE 3" FROM THE END.

BOLT EACH CORNER WITH A $\frac{1}{2}$"×4" GALV. CARRIAGE BOLT.

NOTCH BOTH PIECES OF 2×4 AT THE TOP OF THE TRIANGLE SIX INCHES FROM THE ENDS, SO THEY FIT INTO EACH OTHER TO FORM A FLUSH JOINT. THEN BORE A $\frac{5}{8}$" DIAM. HOLE IN THE CENTER OF EACH NOTCH, AND SCREW TO THE TREE WITH A LAG SCREW.

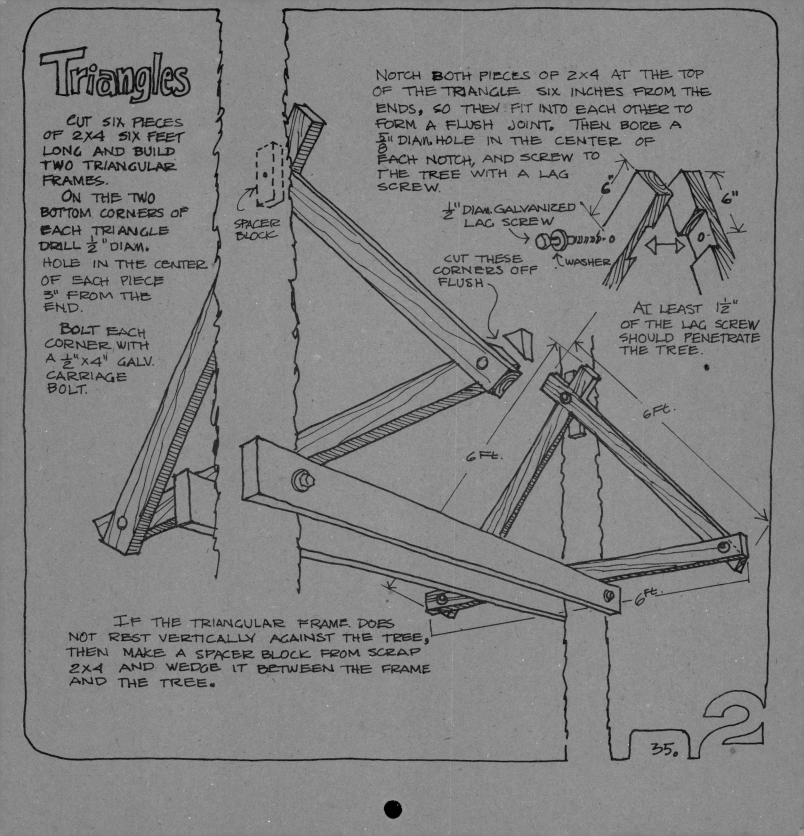

SPACER BLOCK

$\frac{1}{2}$" DIAM. GALVANIZED LAG SCREW

WASHER

6"

6"

CUT THESE CORNERS OFF FLUSH

AT LEAST $1\frac{1}{2}$" OF THE LAG SCREW SHOULD PENETRATE THE TREE.

6 FT.

6 FT.

6 FT.

6 FT.

IF THE TRIANGULAR FRAME DOES NOT REST VERTICALLY AGAINST THE TREE, THEN MAKE A SPACER BLOCK FROM SCRAP 2×4 AND WEDGE IT BETWEEN THE FRAME AND THE TREE.

2

35.

FRAME THE STRUCTURE AS SHOWN HERE
USING 2X4s FOR THE FLOOR FRAME AND 2X3s
FOR THE WINDOW FRAME.

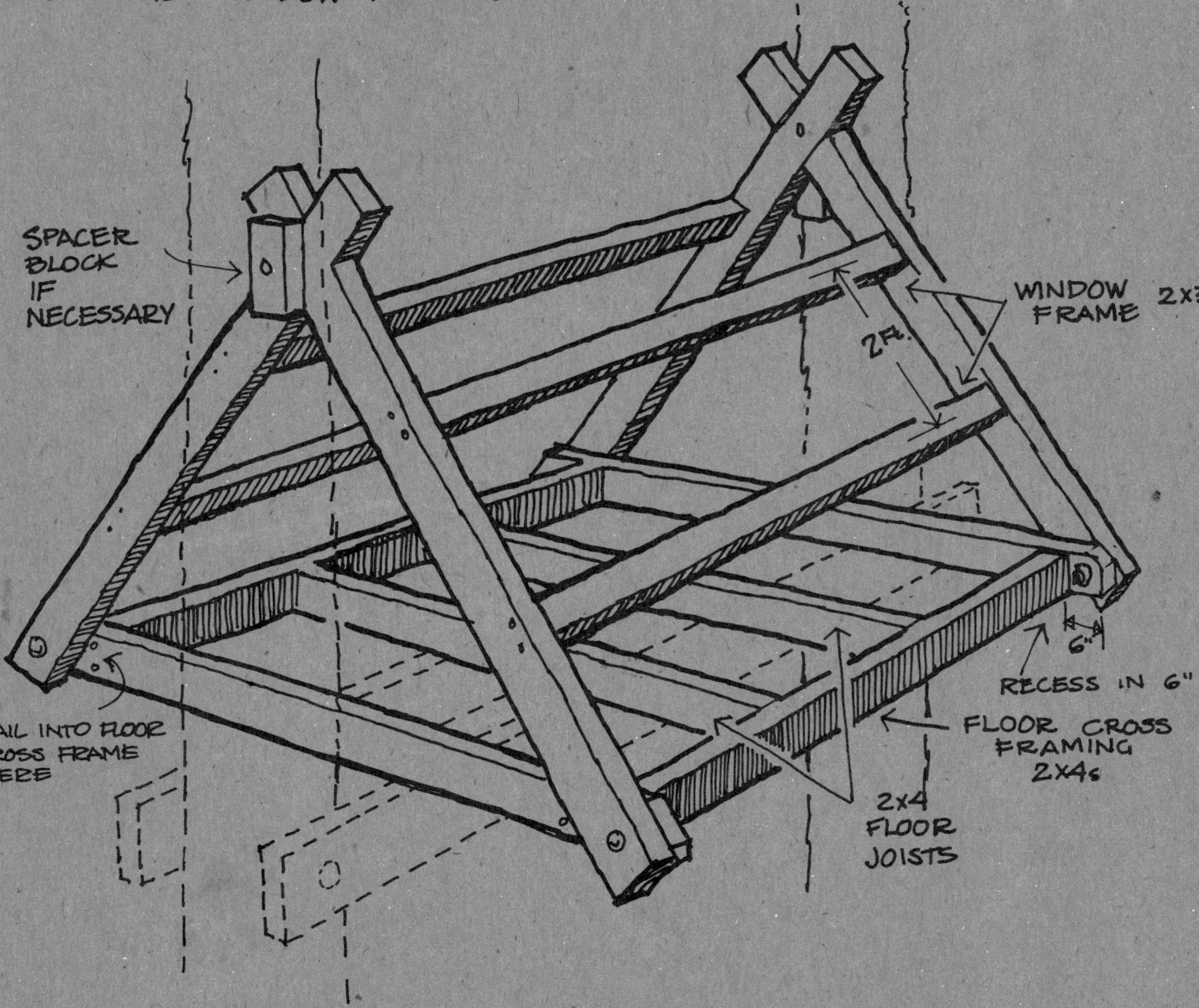

SPACER
BLOCK
IF
NECESSARY

WINDOW
FRAME 2X3s

2FT.

NAIL INTO FLOOR
CROSS FRAME
HERE

RECESS IN 6"

FLOOR CROSS
FRAMING
2X4s

2X4
FLOOR
JOISTS

6"

2

FLOOR & WALLS

FLOOR AND END PANELS
ARE CUT FROM TWO $\frac{3}{4}$"
EXTERIOR GRADE PLYWOOD
SHEETS.

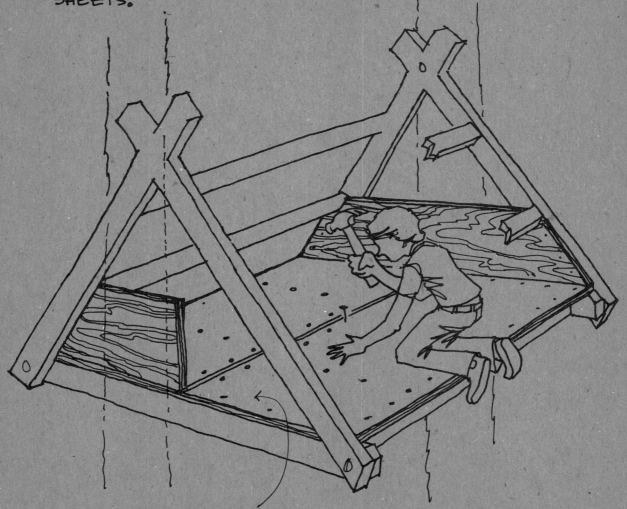

USE 2" GALVANIZED
FINISHING NAILS.

ROOF

THE ROOF IS MADE FROM THREE 4x8 SHEETS OF PLYWOOD SHEATHING CUT IN HALF TO MAKE SIX PIECES 2 Ft. WIDE.

OVERLAP THE TAR PAPER — BUT NOT THE SHINGLES — SO THAT THE WINDOW CAN OPEN AND CLOSE.

TAR PAPER

ASPHALT SHINGLES

OUTER EDGE OF WINDOW REINFORCED WITH 1x4.

2 Ft.

2 Ft.

1x4 PROP

2 Ft.

$\frac{5}{8}$" PLYWOOD SHEATHING CUT INTO 2 Ft. WIDE PANELS.

HAND HOLD, CUT IN FLOOR, MAKES IT EASIER AND SAFER TO CLIMB UP THE LADDER.

12"

PERMANENT LADDER MADE FROM 2x4s AND 1$\frac{3}{8}$" DIAM. DOWELS.

3 Trees

Quite often you can find three trees growing 5 to 6 feet from each other. This is one way you can build a tree house using three trees. You can use logs plus sawn lumber, as shown here, or whatever you have available.

3

You will need at least 13 straight logs, long enough to span the distance between the trees, plus 6" additional on each end. ROUND fence posts are excellent and can be bought at a nursery, but they are expensive.

Using the largest logs first, bore a hole for the lag screw.

6" MIN.

Washer

Lag Screw 6" to 8" long ½" Diameter

40.

3

Start the lag screw by hammering it through the post and into the tree. Give it several hard whacks, then a quarter turn with a wrench. Continue alternating hammering and turning until the screw is all the way in.

If you are screwing into hardwood, you will need to pre-drill a pilot hole slightly less than the screw diameter.

If you are working up high, you may need to prop the other end up using a forked stick like this.

41.

3

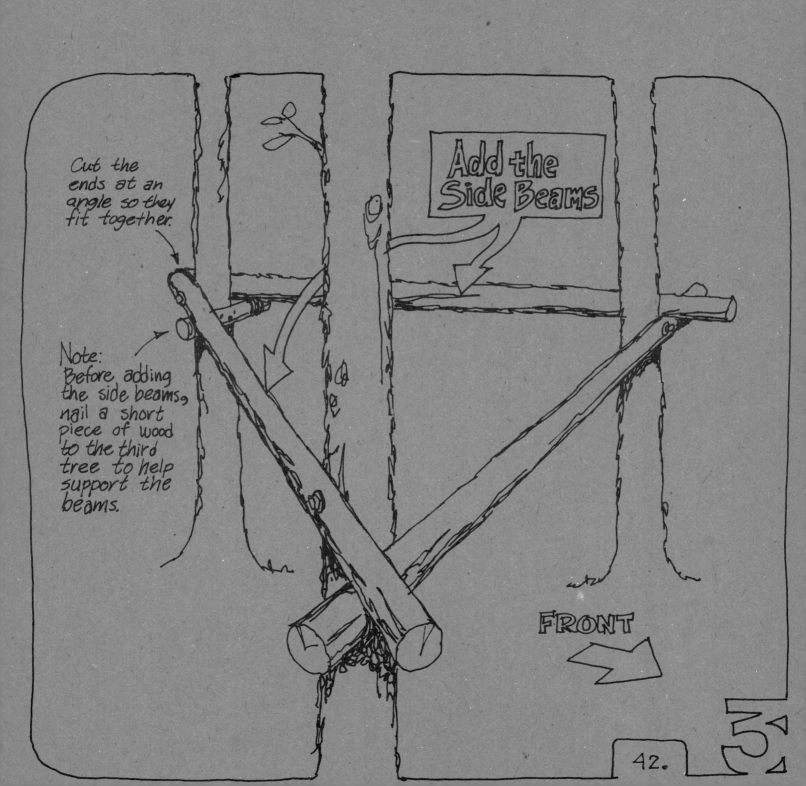

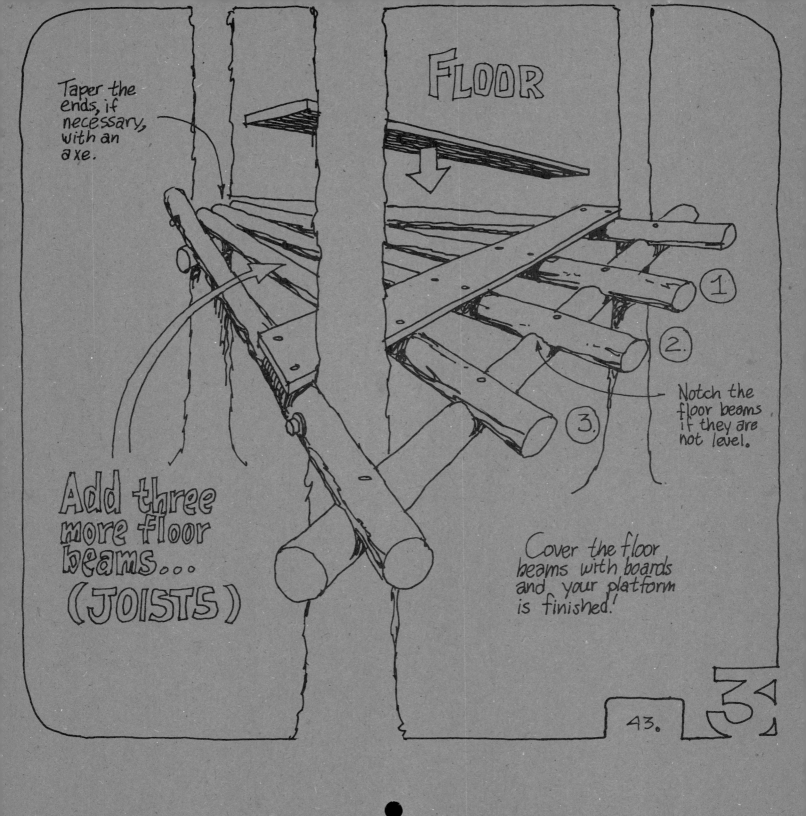

Taper the ends, if necessary, with an axe.

FLOOR

① 1

② 2.

Notch the floor beams if they are not level.

③ 3.

Add three more floor beams... (JOISTS)

Cover the floor beams with boards and your platform is finished!

43.

3

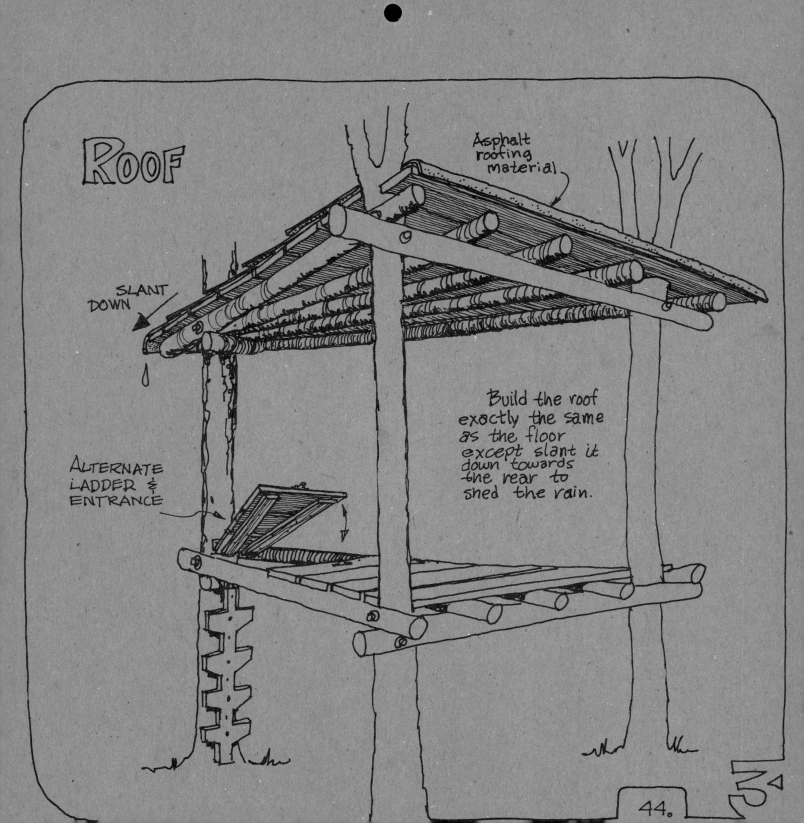

Roof

Asphalt roofing material

SLANT DOWN

Build the roof exactly the same as the floor except slant it down towards the rear to shed the rain.

ALTERNATE LADDER & ENTRANCE

WALLS

Nail the wall boards from the <u>inside</u> at the <u>top</u> and from the <u>outside</u> at the <u>bottom</u>.

This prevents the water from seeping in at the floor.

45.

3

Rope Railing

Manila rope is OK to use here since it's not under severe strain. It also looks better and is cheaper than nylon rope.

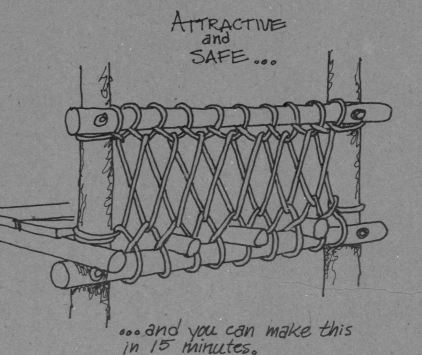

ATTRACTIVE and SAFE...

...and you can make this in 15 minutes.

STEP 1.

Make continuous <u>LOOSE</u> loops around the top rail 4" apart.

← 4" →

STEP 2.
On the bottom rail make loops identical to the loops on the top rail.

STEP 3.
Weave a third rope through the top and bottom loops, skipping every other one, and then weave back through the loops that were skipped.

3

4 TREES

or 2 Trees and 2 Posts

47.

4.

THE POSTS

FIND TWO TREES APPROXIMATELY FOUR TO FIVE FEET APART.
MEASURE SIX FEET OUT FROM THE TREES TO FORM A RECTANGLE
OR SQUARE. BEFORE INSTALLING THE POSTS
IN THE GROUND MAKE SURE EVERYTHING IS
SQUARE BY MEASURING THE DIAGONAL
DISTANCES BETWEEN THE POSTS.
(THEY SHOULD BE THE SAME.)

6 FT.

8 FT.

2 FT.

DIAGONALS
(EQUAL)

TREES
FOUR TO FIVE
FEET APART

FOR INSTRUCTIONS ON
INSTALLING POSTS
SEE PAGE 59

4X4
RED WOOD
POST
(CONSTRUCTION GRADE)

48.

4

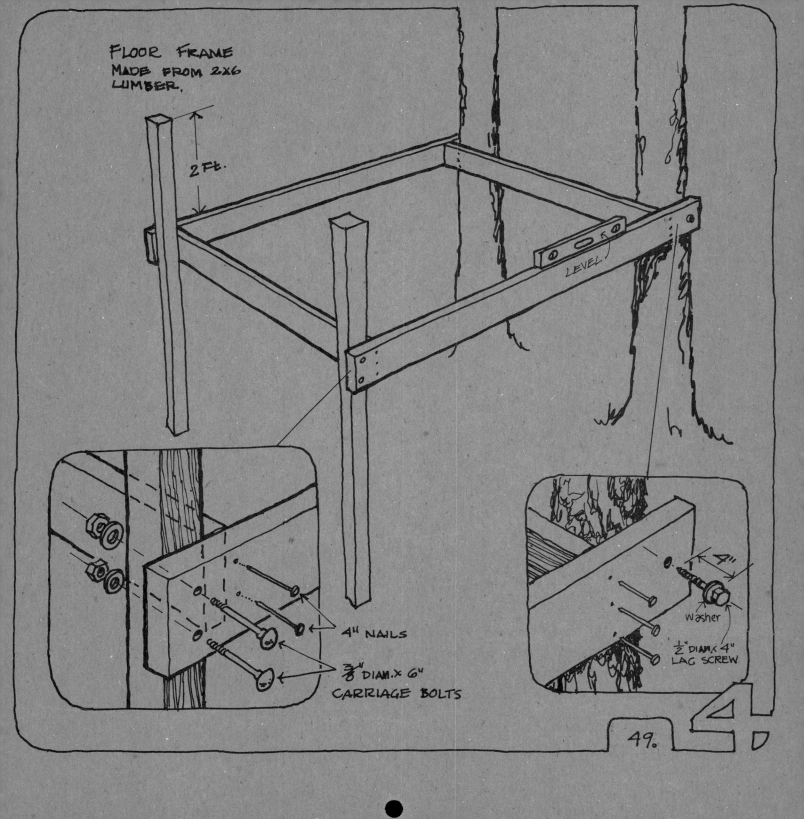

FLOOR FRAME
MADE FROM 2x6
LUMBER.

2 Ft.

LEVEL

4" NAILS

$\frac{3}{8}$" DIAM. x 6"
CARRIAGE BOLTS

4"

Washer

$\frac{1}{2}$" DIAM x 4"
LAG SCREW

49.

FLOOR PLATFORM

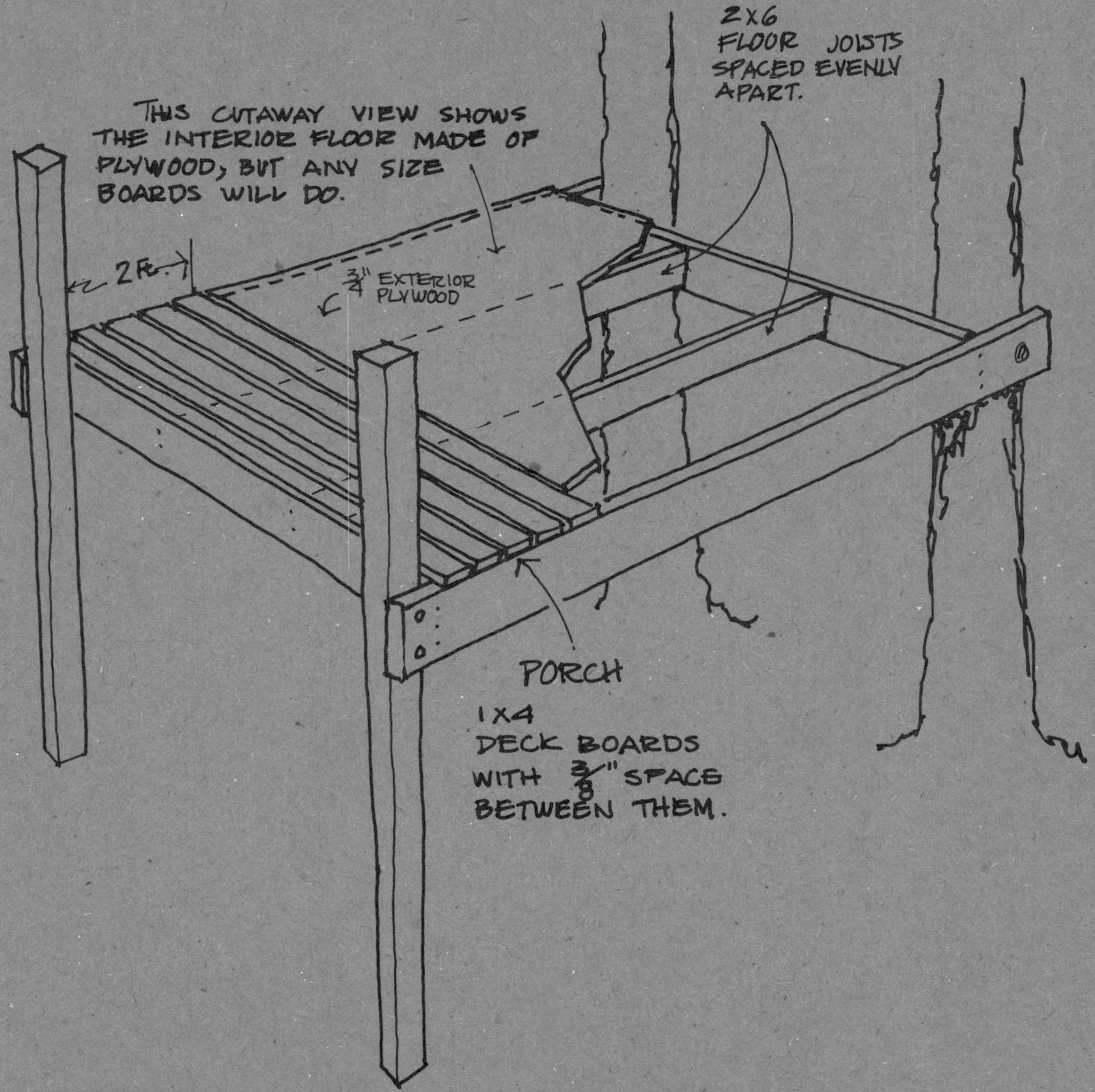

THIS CUTAWAY VIEW SHOWS
THE INTERIOR FLOOR MADE OF
PLYWOOD, BUT ANY SIZE
BOARDS WILL DO.

2X6
FLOOR JOISTS
SPACED EVENLY
APART.

← 2 FT. →

$\frac{3}{4}$" EXTERIOR
PLYWOOD

PORCH

1X4
DECK BOARDS
WITH $\frac{3}{8}$" SPACE
BETWEEN THEM.

50.

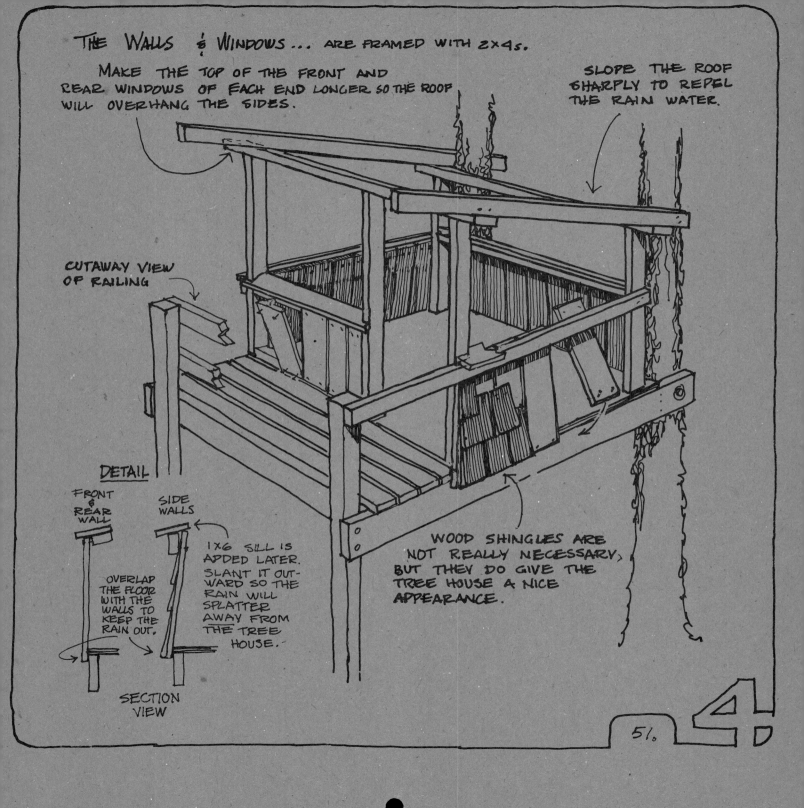

THE WALLS & WINDOWS... ARE FRAMED WITH 2x4s.

MAKE THE TOP OF THE FRONT AND REAR WINDOWS OF EACH END LONGER SO THE ROOF WILL OVERHANG THE SIDES.

SLOPE THE ROOF SHARPLY TO REPEL THE RAIN WATER.

CUTAWAY VIEW OF RAILING

DETAIL

FRONT & REAR WALL

SIDE WALLS

OVERLAP THE FLOOR WITH THE WALLS TO KEEP THE RAIN OUT.

1x6 SILL IS ADDED LATER. SLANT IT OUT-WARD SO THE RAIN WILL SPLATTER AWAY FROM THE TREE HOUSE.

SECTION VIEW

WOOD SHINGLES ARE NOT REALLY NECESSARY, BUT THEY DO GIVE THE TREE HOUSE A NICE APPEARANCE.

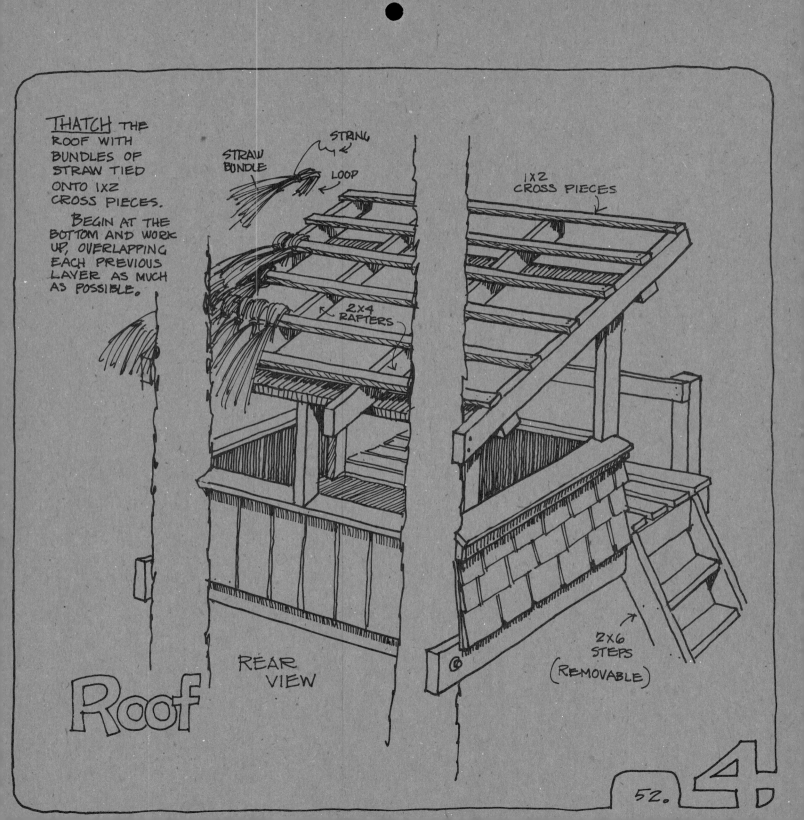

THATCH THE
ROOF WITH
BUNDLES OF
STRAW TIED
ONTO 1X2
CROSS PIECES.

BEGIN AT THE
BOTTOM AND WORK
UP, OVERLAPPING
EACH PREVIOUS
LAYER AS MUCH
AS POSSIBLE.

STRING

STRAW
BUNDLE

LOOP

1X2
CROSS PIECES

2X4
RAFTERS

REAR
VIEW

2X6
STEPS
(REMOVABLE)

Roof

SECTION
IV

MISCELLANEOUS

53.

extra Tips

TOOLS CAN GET LOST VERY EASILY IN THE WOODS; SO CLEAR THE AREA THAT YOU WILL BE WORKING IN OF LEAVES AND TWIGS BEFORE YOU BEGIN. AS AN ADDED PRECAUTION, SPRAY THE HANDLES OF YOUR TOOLS WHITE, OR WRAP A PIECE OF BRIGHT RED TAPE AROUND THEM.

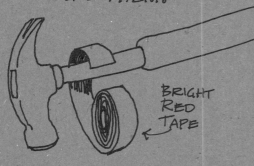

BRIGHT RED TAPE

SPRAY FOR MOTHS AND INSECTS EARLY IN THE SUMMER SO THEY WONT BUILD NESTS IN THE TREE HOUSE.

IT IS VERY HANDY TO HAVE SOMETHING TO HOLD ON TO WHEN YOU ARE CLIMBING INTO A TREE HOUSE. A HAND HOLD CUT IN THE FLOOR CAN SERVE THIS PURPOSE.

HAND HOLD

TREE HOUSES HAVE A WAY OF GETTING DIRTY VERY FAST. KEEP A SMALL WISK BROOM HANGING FROM A NAIL AND BUILD A TRASH DOOR FOR SWEEPING OUT STICKS, LEAVES, AND DIRT.

PLEASE HELP KEEP OUR TREE HOUSE CLEAN

THANK YOU

WASTE

Rope Bridge

If you are lucky enough to have more than one tree house, here is how you can bridge the gap.

55.

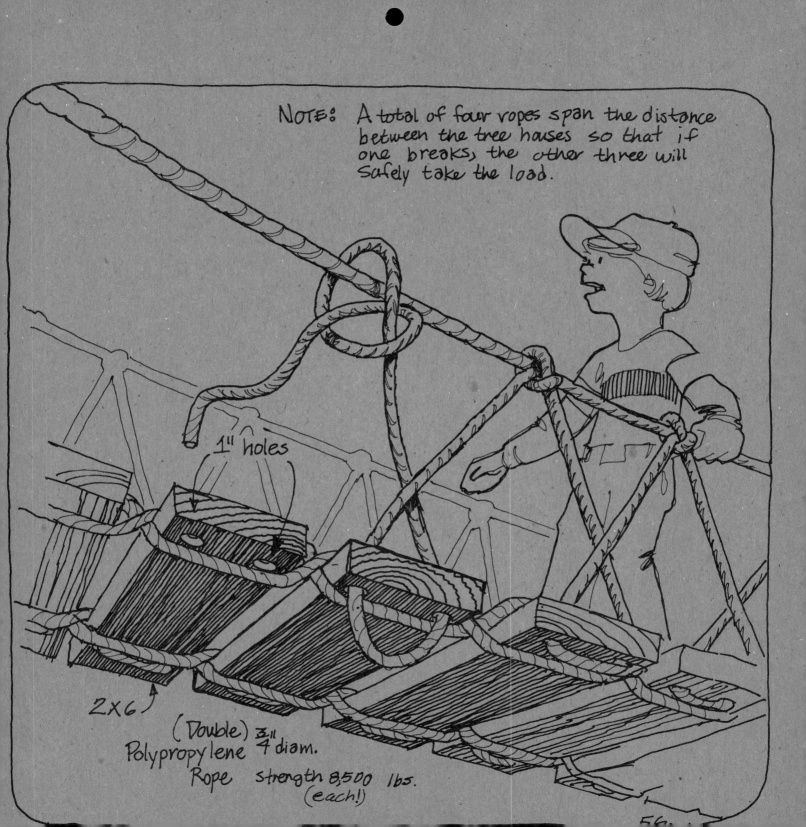

Crow's Nest

FIND A STRONG BRANCH ON A TREE
THAT IS AT LEAST 10 INCHES THICK.
CHOOSE A PLACE THAT IS LEVEL — WHERE
TWO BRANCHES FORK OUT FROM THE MAIN
BRANCH, AND NAIL A HALF BARREL TO THE
BRANCHES. USING 2X6 LUMBER AND 3/4"
EXTERIOR PLYWOOD, BUILD STEPS LEADING UP
TO THE BARREL AS SHOWN HERE.

2X6

3/4"
EXTERIOR
PLYWOOD

ROOFS

MOST WOODEN ROOFS SHOULD HAVE SOME SORT OF FINISHED COVERING APPLIED TO KEEP OUT THE RAIN. ORDINARY TAR PAPER IS USUALLY SUFFICENT FOR MOST TREE HOUSES AND WILL LAST SEVERAL YEARS.

FOR A MORE DURABLE SOLUTION USE ROLLED ROOFING, WHICH IS HEAVIER, OR ASPHALT SHINGLES.

FOR A TRULY ELEGANT ROOF (AND TRULY EXPENSIVE) USE WOOD SHINGLES OR SHAKES.

ANOTHER TYPE OF ROOF (BOARD & BATTEN) DOES NOT REQUIRE ANY FINISHED COVERING IF THERE IS A STEEP PITCH TO THE ROOF.

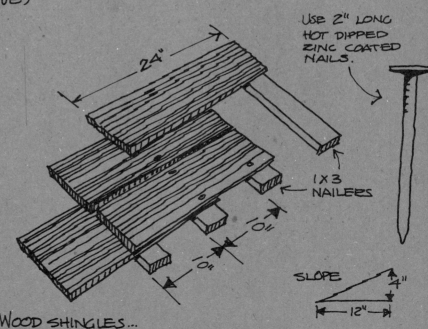

TAR PAPER OR ROLLED ROOFING

SLANT THE ROOF SO THE RAIN WILL RUN OFF EASILY.

OVERLAP EACH LAYER BY ONE HALF THE WIDTH OF THE ROLL.

DRIP LIP

BEND THE ROOFING MATERIAL DOWN OVER THE LOWEST EDGE OF THE ROOF TO FORM A DRIP LIP.

USE 2" LONG HOT DIPPED ZINC COATED NAILS.

24"

1X3 NAILERS

6"

6"

6"

SLOPE

4"

12"

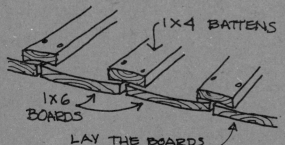

1X4 BATTENS

1X6 BOARDS

LAY THE BOARDS SO THE END GRAIN IS AS SHOWN ABOVE.

WOOD SHINGLES...
...ARE ONLY RECOMMENDED FOR ROOFS WITH A SLOPE OF 4" TO 12".

Posts

IF YOU PLAN ON USING POSTS TO BUILD YOUR TREE HOUSE, HERE ARE SOME FACTS TO KEEP IN MIND.

PRACTICALLY ANY POST WHICH IS PARTIALLY BURIED IN THE GROUND IS NOT LIKELY TO LAST LONG UNLESS PROTECTED FROM <u>DRY ROT</u> AND <u>TERMITES</u>. THIS IS NATURE'S WAY OF RETURNING ALL ORGANIC MATERIAL BACK INTO ITS ORIGINAL STATE IN ORDER TO PROVIDE NOURISHMENT FOR NEW PLANTS. IT IS UP TO YOU TO TAKE MEASURES TO STOP THIS NATURAL TRANSITION, OTHERWISE YOUR POSTS MAY BE REDUCED TO A PULPY MUSH IN LESS THAN A YEAR.

THE BEST PRECAUTION IS TO USE A ROT RESISTANT TYPE OF WOOD, AND ONE NOT ACCEPTABLE TO THE PALATE OF TERMITES AND OTHER WOOD BORERS. THESE ARE, IN ORDER OF PREFERENCE, LOCUST, RED WOOD, CYPRESS, AND CEDAR. UNLESS YOU ARE LUCKY ENOUGH TO FIND LOCUST, YOU WILL PROBABLY HAVE TO SETTLE FOR 4 X 4 CONSTRUCTION TYPE REDWOOD WHICH SHOULD OUTLAST ONE GENERATION OF CHILDREN. INSPECT THE POSTS BEFORE BUYING THEM, TO MAKE SURE THERE ARE NOT TOO MANY KNOTS CONCENTRATED IN ONE AREA.

ADDITIONAL PRECAUTIONS WHICH WILL INSURE THAT THE TREE HOUSE WILL LAST LONG ENOUGH FOR YOUR GRANDCHILDREN TO ENJOY ARE FOUND ON THE NEXT PAGE.

USE ROT RESISTANT WOOD...
...OR SOAK THE POST
OVERNIGHT IN WOOD
PRESERVATIVE CONTAINING
PENTA CHLOROPHENOL.

SOME (OR ALL)
OF THESE PRECAUTIONS
CAN BE TAKEN TO
KEEP THE POST FROM
ROTTING IN THE GROUND.

MAXIMUM STABILITY IS
NECESSARY WHERE THE
POST EMERGES FROM THE
GROUND. DIG OUT A 2 FT.
DIAMETER HOLE 4" DEEP
AND POUR ONE 80 LB. BAG
OF PREMIXED CONCRETE
MIXED WITH WATER INTO
IT.

COVER THE BOTTOM
OF THE POST WITH
TAR AND WHILE IT
IS STILL WET, WRAP
IT IN A PLASTIC
SHEET.

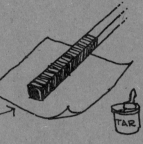

TAR

AFTER A FEW MONTHS A CRACK
WILL APPEAR HERE DUE TO SHRINKAGE
OF THE WOOD. SEAL THE CRACK
WITH BUTYL CAULKING.

4"

THIS DISTANCE
SHOULD BE
BELOW THE
FROST LINE.

EARTH
BACK-
FILL

HERE IS A NEAT
TRICK TO KEEP WATER
FROM SOAKING INTO THE
END GRAIN OF THE
POST THROUGH
CAPILLARY
ACTION.

TAMP DOWN THE
BACK FILL.

PUT A FLAT ROCK
AT THE BOTTOM AND
FILL THE HOLE WITH
SMALL ROCKS TO
PROVIDE GOOD
DRAINAGE.

HEAT THE END OF THE
POST WITH A BLOW TORCH
AND MELT CANDLE
WAX INTO IT.

Tree House Furniture

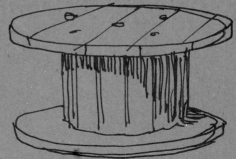

SPOOL... used by Utility Companies to wrap cable, can often be found at dumps.

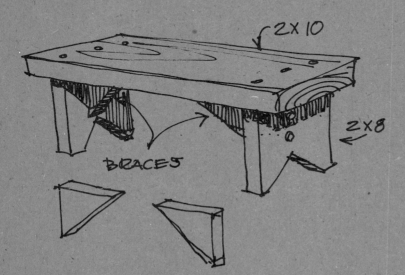

2X10

BRACES

2X8

SCRAP PLYWOOD

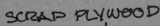
FRONT

FRUIT BOX

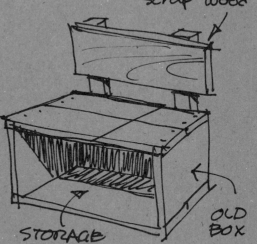

scrap wood

STORAGE

OLD BOX

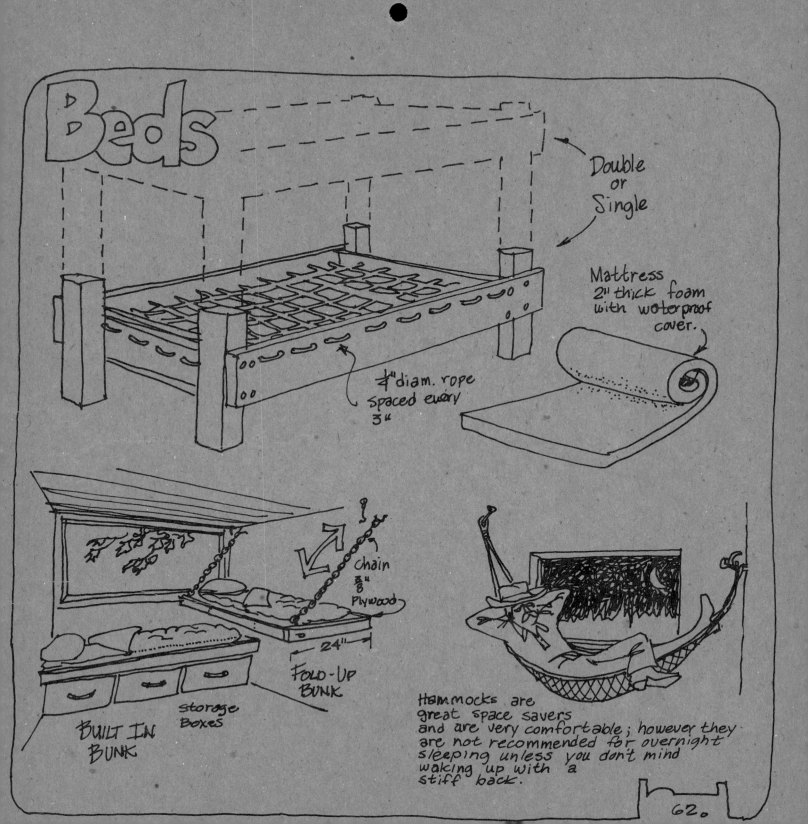

Beds

Double or Single

Mattress 2" thick foam with waterproof cover.

1/4"diam. rope spaced every 3"

chain 3/8" Plywood

24"

FOLD-UP BUNK

BUILT IN BUNK

storage Boxes

Hammocks are great space savers and are very comfortable; however they are not recommended for overnight sleeping unless you don't mind waking up with a stiff back.

Flags

MAKE YOUR OWN.
ANY MATERIAL WILL DO,
BUT NYLON WILL LAST
LONGER.

Oval Rope hole

BRONZE EYE SNAP

REINFORCED EDGE SEAM

THE AVERS'

BRASS GROMMET

MAKE YOUR OWN PULLEY

peg

$\frac{3}{4}''$ DOWEL
IN $\frac{7}{8}''$ HOLE

If you don't want to build a tree house,
here is another way to use the tree.

65.

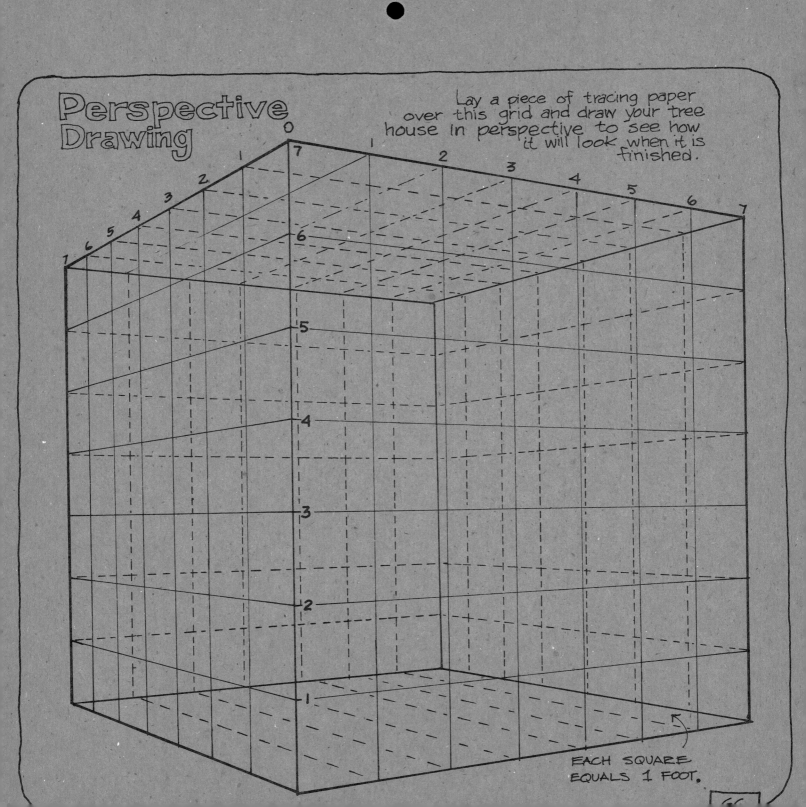

Perspective Drawing

Lay a piece of tracing paper over this grid and draw your tree house in perspective to see how it will look when it is finished.

EACH SQUARE EQUALS 1 FOOT.

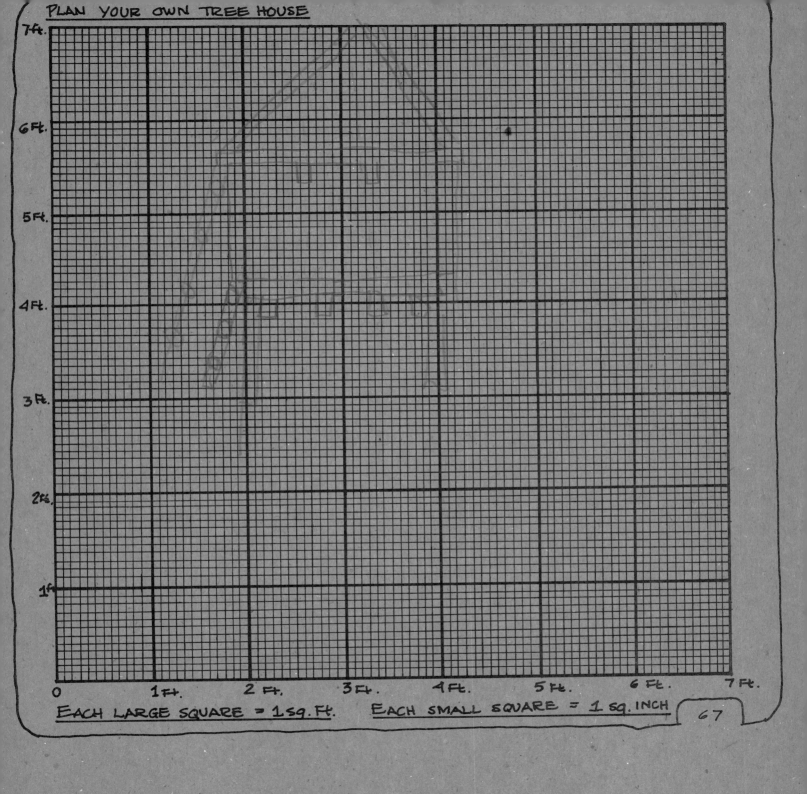

PLAN YOUR OWN TREE HOUSE

EACH LARGE SQUARE = 1 SQ. FT.   EACH SMALL SQUARE = 1 SQ. INCH

67

Deed

Whereas these premises have outlived their usefulness, I hereby deed this property to...

check one

- ☐ my little sister
- ☐ my little brother
- ☐ my little neighbor
- ☐ any kid who wants it.

_____   _____
Signed   Date

68

Building Permit

Permission is hereby granted to
_____ -architect-builder, at
the location of _____ .
to construct, in the best manner
possible, this tree house so that it
will be both pleasing to the eye
and safe to all who occupy its
quarters.

seal of good tree house Construction

signed _____
Parent

_____
Neighbor

_____
Builder

69.

the Tree House Club

Be it known that the following persons are tried and trusted members of the Tree House Club:

1. _ _ _ _ _ _ _ _ _ _ _ _ _ _ President
2. _ _ _ _ _ _ _ _ _ _ _ _ _ _ Vice President
3. _ _ _ _ _ _ _ _ _ _ _ _ _ Treasurer
4. _ _ _ _ _ _ _ _ _ _ _ _ Secretary of State
5. _ _ _ _ _ _ _ _ _ _ _ _ Secretary of Defense
6. _ _ _ _ _ _ _ _ _ _ _ _ Mascot

70.

You're Welcome

Please feel free to use our tree hut. We are very proud of it and hope you like it too. Please help keep it neat and tidy.

_____
owner

71.

BEWARE

72.

Tree Houses, are great for protecting you from Bullies, Skunks, ferocious dogs and creepy crawlies.

73.

Acknowledgements

I WOULD LIKE TO THANK JEANIE (MY WIFE) FOR HER CONSTANT ENCOURAGEMENT, SUSAN MOLDOW (MY EDITOR) FOR HER INFINITE WISDOM, HARRY BURRY, PROFESSOR OF WOOD UTILIZATION, COLLEGE OF ENVIRONMENTAL SCIENCE AND FORESTRY, SYRACUSE, NEW YORK, FOR HIS TECHNICAL INFORMATION, AND ARCHITECT AL KENNERLY FOR HIS INSPIRATION AND KINDNESS.

I WOULD ALSO LIKE TO THANK RICHARD BRENNER, VITO MANNINA, DIANE O'CONNOR AND EVERYONE AT AVON BOOKS FOR THEIR ASSISTANCE IN PREPARING THIS BOOK.

DAVID STILES